Demented

RUTH PIELOOR

CURRENCY PRESS
The performing arts publisher

THE Q
QUEANBEYAN
PERFORMING
ARTS
CENTRE

CURRENT THEATRE SERIES

First published in 2022
by Currency Press Pty Ltd,
PO Box 2287, Strawberry Hills, NSW, 2012, Australia
enquiries@currency.com.au
www.currency.com.au

Typeset by Brighton Gray for Currency Press.
Cover design by Peter Pieloor; cover photography by Jane Duong, featuring
Chrissie Shaw.

Currency Press acknowledges the Traditional Owners of the Country on which
we live and work. We pay our respects to all Aboriginal and Torres Strait
Islander Elders, past and present.

A catalogue record for this
book is available from the
NATIONAL
LIBRARY   National Library of Australia
OF AUSTRALIA

Contents

Theatre Program at the end of the playtext

To Mum, Gran, and Aunty Susan.
May you all be together on a beach in heaven somewhere.

'All women become like their mothers. That is their tragedy.'
Oscar Wilde

Demented was first produced by Ruth Pieloor, in association with Rebus Theatre, at the Q Theatre, Queanbeyan Performing Arts Centre on 11 Aug 2022, with the following cast:

MAGGIE 1 / RACHEL 2 / KAT 2 / DOCTOR	Chrissie Shaw
RACHEL 1 / MAGGIE 2 / KAT 3 / CARER 1 / SUPERVISOR / NURSE	Heidi Silberman
KAT 1 / MAGGIE 3 / RACHEL 3 / CARER 2 / MOTHER / GIRL / LUCY	Rachel Pengilly
EMILY / SHOP ASSISTANT / INGRID / DENTAL NURSE / VOICE	Carolyn Eccles

Director, Ali Clinch
Dramaturg, Peter Matheson
Set Designer, Mel Davies
Lighting Designer, Jacob Aquilina
Costume Designer, Fiona Leach
Puppetry Designer, Hilary Talbot
Sound Designer, Damian Ashcroft
Sound Assistant, Ruth O'Brien
Clowning Consultant, Robin Davidson
Puppetry Director, Ruth Pieloor
Stage Manager, Mel Davies
Assistant Stage Manager and Set construction, Lachlan Davies
Auslan interpreter, Brett Olzen
Production Manager/Producer: Ruth Pieloor

Demented is supported by ArtsACT and the Q Theatre Queanbeyan 'Q the Locals', and in 2021 it was developed with the support of ArtsACT, and Ainslie and Gorman Arts Centres.

CHARACTERS

MAGGIE 1, in her 80s—present day. She is a former circus performer living with dementia. Rachel's mother, Kat's grandmother, Emily's great grandmother.

MAGGIE 2, in her 20s—past.

MAGGIE 3, in her 30s—past.

RACHEL 1, aged 55 years—present day. She is recently divorced, caring, responsible. Fears her own diagnosis. Maggie's daughter, Kat's mum. Emily's grandma.

RACHEL 2, in her 20s—past.

RACHEL 3, aged 54 years old—recent past.

KAT 1, aged 35 years—present day. She has recently returned home to Canberra following the loss of her partner. Emily's mum. Maggie's granddaughter, Rachel's daughter.

KAT 2, aged 29—past, pregnant with Emily.

KAT 3, aged 34—recent past.

EMILY, 5 years old—present day. She is playful, resilient, coming to terms with her new life without a father. Kat's daughter. Rachel's granddaughter, Maggie's great granddaughter.

ANGELA, a silent puppet. Magic realism element in the play, symbolising a friendly Angel of Death, operated by various available cast members.

Other characters: GIRL, MOTHER, CARERS, SHOP ASSISTANT, SUPERVISER, LUCY, INGRID, DENTAL NURSE, DOCTOR, NURSE, LANIE and FRIENDS (on Zoom).

SETTING

The design of the play should be able to accommodate swift transitions between multiple locations.

NOTES

The clowning devices serve to build empathy by intentionally breaking the fourth wall as much as possible, in order to connect with the audience. The life-size child puppet ANGELA is bunraku in style and can take one, two or three people to operate.

Demented can be staged with a minimum cast of three. It is suggested that the actor who plays MAGGIE 1 also plays EMILY, and the actor who plays KAT 1 can play all minor characters, except minor characters in scenes 1, 7, 12, and 21, where there is an option for these 'offstage' characters to be pre-recorded as voiceovers.

This play text went to press before the end of rehearsals and may differ from the play as performed.

PROLOGUE

A: 'GOODBYE MAGGIE'

MAGGIE *lies propped up on her bed with her eyes looking up at the ceiling, her mouth gently open.*

RACHEL *and* KAT *sit by her side.*

Silence.

KAT *and* RACHEL *look at each other, and back to* MAGGIE.

B: 'MAGGIE LEAVES'

Silence.

MAGGIE *lies as before, but her eyes and mouth are now closed.*

ANGELA *sits on the bed watching* MAGGIE.

ANGELA *touches* MAGGIE *delicately.*

Music.

MAGGIE *opens her eyes and looks at* ANGELA. ANGELA *points to the audience with one hand, then offers her other hand to* MAGGIE. MAGGIE *contemplates audience, and nods at* ANGELA *that she is ready.*

ANGELA *hops off the bed, and walks towards audience then stops and looks back at* MAGGIE. ANGELA *waits.* MAGGIE *removes the bedcovers and stands, then walks to* ANGELA *and takes her hand. They stand hand in hand together looking at the audience. They walk towards the audience deliberately in unison.*

We hear a seagull.

MAGGIE *looks upward and smiles, watched by* ANGELA.

ACT ONE

SCENE ONE: 'ICE CREAM'

Dementia ward.

All three performers are on stage, lit in isolation. MAGGIE *stands centre. They talk to other imagined characters, looking at them as if there was someone else next to them.*

A VOICEOVER *of a carer.*

The actors play MAGGIE *during different times of her life.*

MAGGIE 1 *stands on her bed, imagining she is up high on a trapeze, whilst talking to her carer.*

MAGGIE 2 *stands, balancing along the edge of a wall at the beach, whilst talking to her beau.*

MAGGIE 3 *stands precariously on a chair, whilst talking to her daughter.*

VOICEOVER: Margaret. I think you better get down from there.

MAGGIES: I'm fine.

MAGGIE 2: And my name is …

MAGGIE 2 *and* MAGGIE 3: Maggie.

MAGGIE 1: Call me Maggie, dear.

VOICEOVER: Maggie. Please. It isn't safe.

MAGGIE 1: Why don't you have double beds here? I'm married you know. Did you know I was a trapeze artist before having kids!

VOICEOVER: Really? I heard you were a writer. Why don't you hop down, and tell me all about it, Mrs Williams … Maggie.

> MAGGIE 1 *mimes taking the hand of her imaginary carer and hops down.*

MAGGIE 1: Not Maggie. I'm … Birdie. Bir-deee!! The Flying Magpie!!

> MAGGIE 1 *mimes performing a trapeze artist entrance and bows to her imaginary fans.*

VOICEOVER: Okay. Fantastic performance. Come on. Show's over …

MAGGIE 1: Well, of course it's *over.* [*To carer*] Why did you make me a clown? [*To the audience*] Because I got pregnant. A clown!

MAGGIE 1 *hops back up on to the bed.*

Hey! Wait.

MAGGIE 1 *imagines climbing a circus rope ladder, ascending the high trapeze. She waves grandly.*

Hey, I can see my roof from here. Wait. Where's my roof gone?

VOICEOVER: You mean the ceiling?

MAGGIE 1: No. Ceiling? Did you know that ceilings are closer if you have a top bunk …

VOICEOVER: Mrs Williams!

MAGGIE 1 *climbs even higher onto her 'trapeze', and poses gracefully.*

Careful …

MAGGIE 2 *relives standing on a beach wall, humming a tune. She is a little drunk but walks and turns with the confidence of a high-wire artist.*

MAGGIE 2: I don't want to be careful. It's not even a two-foot drop. And it's only beach sand. Live a little. And call me Marg.

VOICEOVER: Come on Marg, let's be helpful friends now and hop down.

MAGGIE 2 *continues playfully on her imaginary beach wall.*

MAGGIE 2: Friends? I thought we were more than friends.
[*Teasingly*] Tell me you love me … Show me … I trust you …

MAGGIE 2 *'stage dives', letting out a squeal of delight.*

Aah!! Let's get married! Have you got a ring?

MAGGIE 1 *checks her hands, and pockets.*

MAGGIE 1: Ring. My ring. Somewhere …

MAGGIE 1 *shares this loss and her distress with the audience.*

I don't know where it's gone …

MAGGIE 3 *stands on tippy toe on a chairs, re-enacting looking through items high up in a cupboard.*

MAGGIE 3: I don't know where it's gone.

VOICEOVER: Okay, Mumma, time to hop down now.

MAGGIE 3: Ya know, if you looked after your things better, I wouldn't have to be up here, would I?! It's not even a valuable ring …

VOICEOVER: Come on. Down we hop.

MAGGIE 3: Well, we are little miss bossy today, aren't we? [*Playfully mimicking the carer's voice*] Down we hop. Hop … [*Asking the audience*] Hop?

> MAGGIE 3 *finally reaches out her hand and is helped down by her imaginary carer.*

VOICEOVER: Let's get you ready.

MAGGIE 3: [*playfully mimicking*] Let's get *you* ready. [*Sharing with the audience*] Oh yes! Kindie!

> MAGGIE 3 *looks around, unsure what to do, then sees a small (imaginary) piece of chalk on the floor. She mimes picking it up, drawing a hopscotch, then throws away the imaginary chalk, and encourages an imaginary girl to play hopscotch.*

Come on. Hop hop.

MAGGIE 1: Hop. Pop … Promise we get an ice cream on the way home. Then I'll hop hop.

> MAGGIE 2 *and* MAGGIE 3 *transform into* CARER 1 *and* CARER 2. *They move from their isolated spots and join* MAGGIE 1 (*now* MAGGIE) *as* CARER 1 *and* CARER 2.

CARER 1: Mrs Williams, please. We don't want you to fall.

MAGGIE: Bir-dee. Fly. Ice cream.

CARER 2: Come on. Let us help you down first. Then, how 'bout an ice cream?

MAGGIE: Promise?

CARER 1: Promise.

> CARER 1 *reaches out a hand towards* MAGGIE.

CARER 2: Promise. Come on, dear.

> CARER 2 *reaches out a hand towards* MAGGIE.

MAGGIE: Ice cream first!

CARER 1: That's right. Ice cream.

CARER 2: Careful …
MAGGIE: Then home.

> CARER 1 *and* CARER 2 *help* MAGGIE *down.*

CARER 2: Well done.
MAGGIE: Birdie did it!
CARER 1: Yes. You did it.
CARER 2: Alright. Let's get you that ice cream.

> CARER 1 *and* CARER 2 *both exit.*

> MAGGIE *sits down on her bed and waits for their return, sharing her delight of the promise of ice cream with the audience.*

> *Silence.*

MAGGIE: [*to audience*] Hello.

> MAGGIE *looks around at her surroundings, finding them unfamiliar.*

Which way is … [*To herself*] home? How do I get out of here?

> MAGGIE *looks around for a door.*

[*To herself*] Where's the … the … um thingy? [*Asks the audience*] You know the ... push … pull … ?

[*Calling offstage*] Where's that ice cream? You promised! [*To herself*] See, I remembered. [*Calling offstage*] Hello? Hello!!

> MAGGIE *realises no-one can hear her. She notices the audience again, but as if for the first time.*

Hello?

> *She smiles at the audience.*

Hell-ooooh.

> MAGGIE *is distracted by a small imagined item on the ground. She wanders over to it and begins to mime playing hopscotch.*

Hop hop hop …

> MAGGIE *'hopscotches' offstage.*

SCENE TWO: 'SEAGULL'

Beach.

MAGGIE *and* RACHEL *are at the beach at the water's edge.*

RACHEL *holds* MAGGIE*'s hand, helping her walk out in the waves.*

MAGGIE *loses her balance and falls on her bottom.* RACHEL *is finally able to help* MAGGIE *to her feet. They walk out of the water together. They arrange themselves on their laid-out beach towels.* RACHEL *does this first and* MAGGIE *copies.*

ANGELA *enters as a young girl with her* MOTHER. MAGGIE *notices* ANGELA *and* MOTHER.

ANGELA *interacts with* MOTHER, *who is focussed only on* ANGELA. ANGELA *looks curiously at* MAGGIE *throughout this scene.* RACHEL *is entirely oblivious to either of them.*

RACHEL *gets out zinc cream and puts some on her nose and cheeks.* RACHEL *passes zinc cream to* MAGGIE, *who, puzzled, looks at the tube of zinc cream and eventually discards it, turning her attention back to* ANGELA *and* MOTHER, *who are miming putting on sunscreen together.*

RACHEL: Oh, I feel like an ice cream now!

> MAGGIE *discovers she has wet sand on her hands and tries to brush it off.*

MAGGIE: Oh! Ah, it's it's … so … sandy!

RACHEL: [*laughing it off*] That's the beach, for you, Mum.

MAGGIE: But I can't get rid of it! It's … its everywhere!

RACHEL: Well, it's just sand …

MAGGIE: Eee-eew! Ugh! Yuck …

RACHEL: Mum. Use your towel? Der.

> RACHEL *sits back with her eyes closed soaking in the sun and breathing in the sea air.* MAGGIE *watches with fascination as* ANGELA *is shown by her* MOTHER *how to use the towel to remove sand.* MAGGIE *begins to copy* ANGELA. *Throughout the scene* MAGGIE *attempts to copy* ANGELA, *then share her 'successes' with* RACHEL, *who sits oblivious with her eyes closed.*

After a time, RACHEL *breaks* MAGGIE*'s concentration.*

Come on, we better get back.

RACHEL starts to get up and gather their things, shaking towels, etc. MAGGIE *notices* ANGELA *and* MOTHER *also preparing to go.* MAGGIE *copies them.* RACHEL *leaves their spot, walking ahead. She sits again to dust her feet more.* MAGGIE *looks at* ANGELA *who copies her* MOTHER *as they sit and dust their feet together.*

Unsure why MAGGIE *is stalling,* RACHEL *gestures and calls to* MAGGIE, *and waits.* MAGGIE *watches* MOTHER *show* ANGELA *how to bang thongs.* ANGELA *shares with* MAGGIE *who joins in too.* MAGGIE *copies* ANGELA*'s actions.* MAGGIE *shares her 'discovery' with* RACHEL, *who is trying not to get impatient.*

RACHEL walks back over to MAGGIE *and hands over her thongs.*

There you go. Bang bang. Dust dust …

MAGGIE: … Dust? Dust …

RACHEL turns to go again. MOTHER *picks up* ANGELA, *who looks at* MAGGIE *and waves.* MAGGIE *smiles and waves back.* RACHEL *is confused who* MAGGIE *is waving to.*

RACHEL: You alright, Mum?

Mum? We'll come back tomorrow before the drive home. We can say goodbye to the beach then, okay?

MAGGIE looks at RACHEL, *then at* ANGELA, *then back to* RACHEL.

Mum?

ANGELA and MOTHER *walk off the beach together.* MOTHER *carries* ANGELA *in her arms.* MAGGIE *watches them go and waves a final goodbye.* ANGELA *waves over her* MOTHER*'s shoulder as they both exit.*

We hear a seagull.

MAGGIE is suddenly distracted by a seagull flying past.

MAGGIE: Oh, look! It's a … a magpie!

MAGGIE checks to see ANGELA *has seen it too, but* ANGELA *has gone.*

RACHEL: Seagull, Mum. We're at the beach …

MAGGIE: [*shouting to seagull*] Hello, Maggie! You were in my most famous short story!

RACHEL: Ya need your glasses, Mum. Seagull. It's a seagull.

> RACHEL *begins to walk off the beach again but stops to check* MAGGIE *is following.* MAGGIE *looks out across the ocean and notices the audience. She looks at them curiously.* RACHEL *waits, concerned.*

Maybe an afternoon nap hey?

> RACHEL *tries to figure what* MAGGIE *is looking at.*

Bye beach. Bye seagull. Come on, Mum …

> RACHEL *goes to leave*

MAGGIE: Why do we? How do we … ?

> MAGGIE *turns about, trying to orientate herself.*

> RACHEL *stops, mildly alarmed.*

RACHEL: Mum?

MAGGIE: How do we … ? Where's the … oh dashit, what's it called … Rachel, you know the …

> MAGGIE *looks at her hand, miming a door.*

The … the door? Door! That's it. Door.

> RACHEL*, realising something is not cognitively 'right' with* MAGGIE*, walks over to her and links arms with* MAGGIE.

RACHEL: Come on Mum. Let's go have a nice hot shower back at our room, okay?

> MAGGIE *walks back with* RACHEL. MAGGIE *keeps pausing to look back at the audience, mouthing 'sea gull' over and over as if she's learned a new word. They continue walking off the beach.* MAGGIE *looks back one last time at her new-found friends—the audience.*

MAGGIE: [*to the audience*] Seagull!

> MAGGIE *smiles and waves at the audience as they both exit.*

SCENE THREE: 'OFF THE COACH'

Bus terminal.

KAT *and* EMILY *enter.* EMILY *leaps straight into* RACHEL*'s arms. They all hug.*

EMILY: [*to* KAT] Look there she is, Mummy ... Rachie Nan!!

RACHEL: Emmeeee!! Oh, you've grown so ...

EMILY: That was the longest bus trip in the whole world!

KAT: Hi Mum.

RACHEL: Darling Kat ... Oh, you're way too thin!

KAT: Mum.

RACHEL: Sorry. Just so glad my baby and her baby are home.

KAT: Mum, we're only ...

EMILY: I held my breath on the stinky-bumpy toilet, and I did two wees and didn't fall in!

RACHEL: Wow. *Two* wees ...

KAT: Definitely flying next time. Where's Dad?

RACHEL: Oh, he's ... we've been having some issues.

KAT: Yeah, I know. You told me, remember. But still ... he's not here? My suitcase is really heavy ...

RACHEL: He's got a place now.

KAT: What?

RACHEL: Well I ... kicked him out.

KAT: Mum?!

RACHEL: I'm sure he'll tell you all about it. That it's me, not him, ... and how we've grown apart blah blah blah. [*To* EMILY] But look how *you've* grown, young lady!

KAT: Why did you ... ? You never mentioned it was *that* bad ... Oh, these ones are ours.

    She grabs the bags.

RACHEL: Well it's been a while, you've had your hands full ... And anyway he's been such an ah ... Intorab ... Intorra-bubb ... In-torr ... intolerable! When did us women start normalising 'grumpy old man syndrome'—just an excuse to be intolerable, if you ask me.

EMILY: Intorri-bubble!

KAT: Sounds like it's just *you* not tolerating *him*, Mum.

RACHEL: Hey, he is mean how he speaks to me, [*to* EMILY] unlike this munchkin.

EMILY: Are you talking about Grandad?

RACHEL: Yes, and he sends kisses …

He said he will see you on the weekend, okay? He's too busy today … being a tired smelly grumpy old man.

KAT: Mum! There's your 'normalising'!

EMILY: / Eww smelly old man.

RACHEL: / Eww, right?! Oh, Em. I have missed you so much, darling. Come here!!

And we will go visit Baggie Nanna later too, okay?

EMILY: Baggie Nanna!!

RACHEL: She misses you very much. [*To* KAT] I have to talk to you about your Nanna. She's … well maybe later. She's always asking after you, you know. Kat this. Kat that …

KAT: Mum. How can you … you kicked him out?

RACHEL: Look, now you're back … we'll get a chance to talk properly, okay?

Oh, Kat darling, you've been doing it so tough since … since Sammy …

EMILY: Are you talking about my daddy?

KAT: Emily, I'm talking to Rache Nan … [*To* RACHEL] Mum, can we …

EMILY: He died of a broken heart!

KAT: Heart failure, darling. Well, technically heart disease while we're being so honest in front of a five-year-old. Mum!

EMILY: Five-and-a-half!

KAT: Mum. It's freezing. Can we just go?

RACHEL: Yes. Sorry. [*To* EMILY] We should be talking about what you want for dinner …

EMILY: Sketti beat malls!

RACHEL: Sketti meat malls?

EMILY: Beat malls! Sketti beat malls! Sketti beat malls!!

EMILY *dances round in circles singing.*

RACHEL: I'm just saying … Dave is Dave, and it's been a long time coming, and … well, he isn't …

KAT: Sammy?

> KAT *starts crying.* RACHEL *hugs her.* EMILY *joins in. They all hug amongst the luggage.*

RACHEL: Sorry, darling girl. Hey … you're home now.

KAT: We're only staying for a couple months, remember?

EMILY: Intorri-bubble! Intorri-bubble!!

RACHEL: I remember. Come on. The car's … ah … um … [*Looking around*] this way. This way!!

> *They all exit.*

SCENE FOUR A: 'BATH'

Maggie's apartment.

MAGGIE *is alone in her apartment. Throughout this sequence* MAGGIE *comfortably shares with the audience her confusion, satisfaction, frustration, curiosity, etc.*

MAGGIE *arrives out of the elevator. Disorientated, and thinking she has gotten out on the wrong floor, she goes back to the elevator (offstage). She enters again (onstage) satisfied she has finally 'arrived' on the correct floor, outside her flat. She comes to her front door and waits. She looks about and presses the doorbell. She waits. She presses the button again and waits. She looks at the audience. She suddenly remembers she has keys and gets them out. She finally opens the door and goes into a dark apartment, instantly tripping on something.*

She finds the light switch. She turns on the light switch. She waits and turns it off again. It seems she thinks she is still in the elevator or waiting for something. She repeats this a few times, eventually forgetting the purpose of the switch.

After a time, she spies her washing basket on the floor and goes over towards it. She stands looking down at it, then suddenly removes some of the clothes from it, takes off her shoes and her jacket and hops into the washing basket as if it was a comfy chair or bed. She tries to get comfortable.

ANGELA *enters.*

MAGGIE: Is that you, Kat? How'd you get in here? Does your mum know you're here? You know you shouldn't be in here when I'm having a bath. Oh, all the bubbles have gone now …

> MAGGIE *tries to cover herself with clothes as 'bubbles'. She notices* ANGELA *has gone. She hops out of the bath and starts drying herself with nearby clothing items. Then feeling cold, she starts putting on various items of clothing on over the top of her other clothes.*
>
> *Doorbell rings.*
>
> MAGGIE *pauses, unsure. She looks to audience for an answer of what to do. She waits, listening, then continues to dress herself more.*
>
> *Doorbell rings again.*
>
> MAGGIE *mimics the sound.*

SCENE FOUR B: 'URN'

Maggie's apartment.

RACHEL: [*calling from offstage*] Mum?!

> RACHEL *and* KAT *enter.*

KAT: [*continuing a conversation*] Well maybe an urn is safer than a kettle, then?

RACHEL: Mum? It's just us. Didn't you hear the doorbell?

> MAGGIE *seems uninterested, still fixated on her clothes.*

Look who's here!

MAGGIE: What are you two doing here, now?

KAT: It's nice to see you too.

> KAT *goes to give* MAGGIE *a huge hug but can only manage a peck on the cheek.*

How've you been, Baggie Nanna? Mum said …

MAGGIE: I was just getting ready for bed.

RACHEL: Look who's here! Aren't you hot, Mum? [*Referring to all the layers of clothes she is now wearing*] Guess what? Kat and Emily are moving back to Canberra, isn't that great?

KAT: Well, just for a month or so, Mum … the start of school term, remember?

RACHEL: And speaking of remember … we're all going for brunch today …

MAGGIE: But it's bedtime …

KAT: [*to* MAGGIE] Baggie Nan, It's ten a.m. In the morning!

RACHEL: Come on, I'll help you get ready.

MAGGIE: And what's this about an urn. Has some one died again? You know you can use your father's urn. It's just sitting there.

KAT: Ah um … Are we ready to go out, then?

RACHEL: Mum. Granddad passed away a few years ago now, remember?

MAGGIE: Oh, darling … of course I … remember. The elephant is in the room!

KAT: [*quietly to* RACHEL] Is Bag Nan okay?

> MAGGIE *looks at audience. She rolls her eyes in reference to all the questions, and goes over to the bookshelf.*

RACHEL: Where have all your shoes gone, Mum?

> MAGGIE *stands in front of the bookshelf, dancing and humming happily to herself.*

KAT: Maybe you two should just go for coffee. I'm still unpacking, and there's a meeting today to volunteer at Emily's school I should probably get to …

> RACHEL *is distracted looking for Maggie's shoes.* MAGGIE *picks up an urn. She opens it and empties the contents straight out on the floor. She puts the lid back on, sharing her cleverness with the audience and reaches out an empty urn to hand to Rachel.*

MAGGIE: There you go.

RACHEL: Mum!!

KAT: Jesus Christ, Nanna!

MAGGIE: It'll save you pennies. They're expensive ya know.

RACHEL: Mum, that's Dad!

> RACHEL *gets a dustpan.* KAT *stands back, covering her face.*

MAGGIE: Oh, Bill won't miss it. It's not as if he needs it anymore.

RACHEL: No, that *is* Dad!

KAT: Far out. My asthma's gunna flare up. I gotta go …

RACHEL: Oh, come on, Kat! Don't just leave. I did warn you she gets confused sometimes.

KAT: We can all go for a coffee another time. I'm back for a while. I actually have to check I signed a school admin form anyway …

> KAT *gathers her things to leave.* RACHEL *is cleaning up ashes as* MAGGIE *is holding the urn in her hand and shouts after her.*

MAGGIE: Don't forget your …

KAT: Nice to see you Baggie Nanna! See you tonight, Mum.

> KAT *exits.*

MAGGIE: You forgot you … your container … thingy!

> *She grabs a photo frame.*

You can have this too if you like darling. Ah … ah um … Kat. [*To herself*] People don't need things anymore when they're dead, silly. [*Asking the audience*] Do they?

RACHEL: [*coughing and trying to put the ashes back in the urn*] No, Mum. Maybe we can all go for a coffee another time, okay?

MAGGIE: [*inspecting a book*] What's this for? Why have I got all these things?

RACHEL: Mum, they're your books.

MAGGIE: They're not mine.

> *She starts throwing them on the floor.* RACHEL *retrieves them.*

RACHEL: Mum!

> Okay. Look. [*Putting books back on the shelf*] Why don't we go for a coffee you and me … now?

MAGGIE: Oh, goody. I thought you'd never ask.

> MAGGIE *grabs her coat.*

[*To* RACHEL] Where's um … ah … Kat? She's always late. Oh, we can meet her there, I guess.

> MAGGIE *smiles knowingly at audience, picks up the kettle and is out the door swiftly.* RACHEL *grabs her handbag, and follows* MAGGIE *out hurriedly.*

SCENE FIVE: 'MAGPIE'

Pet shop.

SHOP ASSISTANT *is behind a counter in a pet shop.* MAGGIE *enters and walks up to her.*

SHOP ASSISTANT: Hello. How may I help you, Mam?

MAGGIE: I would like to buy a … a … black and white bird, please.

SHOP ASSISTANT: Oh. We've got some budgies that have *grey* and white …

MAGGIE: Magpie. That's it. That's what they're called. I remembered. Magpie.

SHOP ASSISTANT: Well … Um … We've got some native birds. They're actually cockatiels … like a parrot.

MAGGIE: No, I want a … you know. That bird that dives from the sky … and sings. You know …

MAGGIE *attempts to make a magpie sound.*

SHOP ASSISTANT: [*slightly amused*] Our canaries are famous for singing. We have one male left.

MAGGIE: [*sharing with the audience*] Is it a magpie?

SHOP ASSISTANT: Well, I wouldn't actually be wanting a magpie. [*Trying to be funny*] It might swoop you!

Beat.

This one's seventy dollars.

MAGGIE: Does that include the cage?

SHOP ASSISTANT: No, the cage is separate. It includes a vaccination and a de-licing treatment.

MAGGIE: I don't want to keep it in a cage. I want it to fly … and sing.

She attempts a magpie sound again.

I want it to be free. Can I have it free without the cage?

SHOP ASSISTANT: I'm sorry, Madam, we can sell you the canary for seventy dollars, but you will need a cage. Or if you already have a cage at home, then some sort of container to take it home in.

MAGGIE: I've got an urn at home.

SHOP ASSISTANT: Excuse me, I'm just going to get my supervisor.

> SHOP ASSISTANT *moves away.* SUPERVISOR *enters.* MAGGIE *waits and watches as* SHOP ASSISTANT *and* SUPERVISOR *whisper and point at her.* MAGGIE *shares with the audience the rudeness of the* SHOP ASSISTANT *and* SUPERVISOR. *Fed up,* MAGGIE *promptly exits.*

SCENE SIX: 'SIGNING FORMS'

Rachel's car.

RACHEL *drives.* KAT *in front passenger seat.* MAGGIE *sits in the back, looking out the window.*

RACHEL: [*to* KAT] But it's not that bad. And I'm happy to help her. She's my mum. Ya know, it's time for me to give back.

KAT: Well, *I* can't be expected to look after her as well as Emily now that …

RACHEL: Please don't give me that 'too busy' single parent crap. I'm just saying … we can't dump her in some home for demented people, Kat, because you think I can't cope, and you're too busy.

MAGGIE: Why's this roundabout still going round?

KAT: No-one calls them demented, Mum.

RACHEL: Alzheimer's. Yeah, yeah, I know.

KAT: And clearly her home care package only does so much, and we won't be just dumping her …

> MAGGIE *leans forward to join in.*

MAGGIE: Are you trying to put me in a home?

KAT *and* RACHEL: No.

RACHEL: See. She doesn't want to go. You don't want to go, do ya Mum?

> MAGGIE *is unsure but nods 'no' in agreement.*

They say it's best to keep them at home for as long …

KAT: Who's 'they', Mum? You said she wanders off!

MAGGIE: Don't put me in a home.

KAT: Can't we at least put her on a waiting list?

MAGGIE: I can wait.

RACHEL: Mum, we're just going down the road to the doctor, okay?

KAT: It can take ages.

MAGGIE: I'm not sick. Stupid waiting rooms.

RACHEL: We'll go straight home after.

MAGGIE: I'm not going to a home.

RACHEL: Your home. I'll take you home.

MAGGIE: Promise?

RACHEL: Yes!

MAGGIE: I want an ice cream.

KAT: We're just seeing if the doctor can help us sign some forms, so we can share permission to look after you, okay?

MAGGIE: Per-mission …

RACHEL: This doesn't feel right.

KAT: God, Mum. Don't you wish you had cleaners and carers and people delivering *you* meals, in a nice home!

MAGGIE: Another roundabout? [*To the audience*] Is this the same roundabout?

KAT: Mum, you're the one who said all the paperwork is overwhelming. And if simple consent forms are too hard for Bag Nan to manage then … I mean soon she won't even be able to make any of those type of decisions …

RACHEL: So, this power of attorney thing. Enduring power. Do we both … ?

MAGGIE: [*to* KAT] What power? [*To* RACHEL] Your brother's an electrician. Is he coming?

KAT *and* RACHEL: No!

RACHEL: We're just trying to help you, Mum.

MAGGIE: I don't need help, or give my per-mission. I haven't even got dementia yet, anyway.

KAT: Jesus! [*To* RACHEL] See?

RACHEL: [*parking the car*] You remember, Mum … ? They said with your dementia, you might start to forget things …

KAT: Start …

MAGGIE: *My* dementia? … Poppy cock.

RACHEL: Okay! And we're here.

KAT: Huh, great park, Mum.

RACHEL: It's okay Mum. We're both with you to help you with all the signing. Okay?

MAGGIE: Oh, a signing. I haven't done a book signing for ages. I hope I can remember how to do it.

[*As if signing a book*] 'Best Wishes, Margaret J. Williams'. See I remember just fine.

They all get out of the car.

Ooh it's hot, shall we go for ice cream on the way home, girls? You promised. See I remember. Come on. Who's got a pen?

KAT *and* RACHEL *follow an eager* MAGGIE *out of the car.* MAGGIE *leads the way miming writing in the air, sharing her excitement with the audience.*

Per-Mission!

They exit.

SCENE SEVEN: 'FRIENDS'

Maggie's apartment.

MAGGIE *and her carer* LUCY *are sitting together on the couch,* MAGGIE *with a tea and biscuit,* LUCY *wearing a surgical mask and disposable gloves.* RACHEL *knocks on door.* LUCY *gets up to answer the door.* MAGGIE *dunks the biscuit in the tea, then attempts to put the whole biscuit in her mouth.*

RACHEL: Oh hi, Lucy. How're you going?

MAGGIE: She's not going. And I'm not going. I've been telling her … I'm not going to a home.

LUCY: Good thanks, Rachel. Your mum's actually having a good day. We got everything done.

RACHEL: Thanks, Lucy. [*To* MAGGIE] Hi Mum. Lucy's gotta go now.

LUCY *gathers her things to leave.*

MAGGIE: Who's Lucy?

RACHEL: Your carer, Lucy. She's just been here with you the last three hours, remember?

MAGGIE: You? Of course, I remember you. [*To* LUCY] Bye Kat, darling.

LUCY: Bye Mrs Williams!

RACHEL: It's Lucy. [*To* LUCY] Thanks, Lucy. Bye.

LUCY *exits.*

MAGGIE: Why'd Kat *leave* so suddenly … ?

RACHEL: Lucy. That was … So, Mum … I brought my laptop!

> RACHEL *sits down on couch next to* MAGGIE. *She opens her laptop.*

Mum. Do you remember, we have a Zoom meeting with your writing group organised for today? Ooh, any minute … Isn't that great? They emailed me the link, so …

MAGGIE: No, you go. I'll stay here.

RACHEL: Come on, it'll be fun!

> RACHEL *opens a Zoom meet with* MAGGIE'*s friends.* MAGGIE *sits to join* RACHEL, *but strains to see.*

MAGGIE: What are you doing?

RACHEL: It's a Zoom meeting.

MAGGIE: What?

RACHEL: Here we go. Hi everyone. We made it.

FRIENDS [*voiceover*]: Hi, Maggie. / It's Maggie, Hi! / Hello, Margaret.

MAGGIE: Agh, hello! Oh wow, there's … um … how did … ?

FRIEND [*voiceover*]: It's Cathy! Hi Maggie. We've missed you.

MAGGIE: Cathy … um, but who's … who's that?

RACHEL: [*pointing at the screen*] There's Peta, and Jasja, and look there's Jo. Hi Joanna!

MAGGIE: Why's everyone so small? I can't see them properly

> MAGGIE *tries to look behind the laptop.*

[*To* RACHEL] Turn it up. I can't hear. Can you … uh hear me?

RACHEL: Sshh … they're starting …

FRIEND [*voiceover*]: Hello all. Welcome to this month's online writing session. We welcome back Maggie and her daughter Rachel, but I'm mindful of time, so we'll get stuck straight in and save chit chat for later. We'll start with Peta's passage. Readings first and feedback at the end, so on mute everyone. Thanks Peta …

> *A voice reading prose in background fades.*

MAGGIE: What's she talking about, Kat?

RACHEL: It's Rachel, and Cathy just explained … Sshh … you're missing Peta's bit.

MAGGIE: What. Tell them to ... [*Shouting*] Speak up!

RACHEL: We're on mute, Mum ... she can't hear you.

MAGGIE: Why can't they hear me? Hello! Oh look, that's ... who's that? Hello! I can't hear a thing!

> MAGGIE *loses interest and sips her tea.*

RACHEL: That's Peta, Mum.

MAGGIE: My tea's cold.

> MAGGIE *gets up and goes to the kettle.*

RACHEL: Mum, we're in the middle of your Zoom meeting.

MAGGIE: Oh, turn that rubbish off. You always did spend too much time on that thing.

> MAGGIE *stands staring at the kettle.*

RACHEL: [*taking herself off mute*] Sorry to interrupt. Ah, Mum and I have to go. It has really meant a lot to us, to see all your faces. Mum loved it.

FRIENDS: [*voiceover*] Thanks Rachel. / Bye Marg. / Bye Maggie!

RACHEL: [*to* MAGGIE] Everyone says bye, Mum. [*To the laptop*] Bye everyone!

> RACHEL *closes the laptop.* MAGGIE *holds the kettle in her hand*

MAGGIE: What are you watching, anyway?

RACHEL: Just friends.

MAGGIE: Friends? [*Scoffs*] American rubbish. Kettle. Where's the kettle?

SCENE EIGHT: 'CAR PARK'

Beach.

RACHEL *and* MAGGIE *in car. They have just arrived at the beach car park on a beautiful day.* MAGGIE *has been left unattended with the zinc cream and has covered her whole face with it, much like clown make-up.*

RACHEL: [*parking the car*] See. I told you if we avoided school holidays it would be less crowded. Wow the waves looks perfect today.

> RACHEL *looks at* MAGGIE.

Oh, Mum. It's just for your nose and cheeks. Here let me rub it off.

MAGGIE: But what do we do here?

RACHEL: [*trying to rub off some zinc cream from Maggie's face*] Well, we'll probably stay just an hour and have lunch then drive back. It was just too hard to pack and everything to stay overnight this time. Hope you don't mind.

MAGGIE: No, no. I mean. What is that? What's it for?
     What do we do?

RACHEL: It's the beach, Mum. Ya know …

MAGGIE: No, no, no, no. It looks … boring. Let's go home.

RACHEL: But we just got here! You love the beach. We've been planning this.

MAGGIE: We can talk on the drive. Come on. Drive! Tell me on the way how's that handsome um … Dave of yours?

RACHEL: He's a shit and I'm leaving him actually, Mum. Remember?

MAGGIE: Never mind. You'll work it out. Go on, drive the bus … ah car. We wanna be home before my favourite TV show.

     She raises her eyebrows knowingly to audience.

What's it called?

     RACHEL *starts rummaging through bags in the back.*

RACHEL: I can record shows for you Mum, and you've got Netflix and Foxtel remember? I'm just going to change into my swimmers in that toilet block there, okay? Will you be okay here?

MAGGIE: Just drive. I don't need the toilet yet. And tell me how's Kat going?

RACHEL: I've just been telling you the last couple of hours!

MAGGIE: Are they still trying for another baby? I hope it's a boy. [*To the audience*] Too many Williams women if you ask me.

     RACHEL *hugs the steering wheel trying to compose herself.*

RACHEL: Mum! Kat's husband passed away a couple of years ago, remember?

MAGGIE: Stop asking me if I remember, and just drive!

RACHEL: Probably best you don't ask Kat about Sammy … passing away I mean.

MAGGIE: You mentioned him passing, not me. And stop asking me if I remember things all the time. I don't have this dementia thing, ya know. Stupid doctors.

RACHEL: Right!

> RACHEL *puts on her seat belt and turns on the engine.*
>
> *The radio blares.*
>
> RACHEL *turns up the volume.* MAGGIE *covers her ears as if in pain, letting out a strained sound.* RACHEL *drives erratically out of car park, with* MAGGIE *thrown about in her seat.*

SCENE NINE: 'HOW MUCH TIME'

Kat's kitchen.

RACHEL *and* KAT *are making cookies together, occasionally watching* EMILY, *who sits on the floor and plays with her dolls.*

KAT: So, you're saying it might be easier if we *both* go with her?

RACHEL: You know how much she loved the beach. Then … like you said, I don't have to do it all on my own.

KAT: Maybe Dad can help.

RACHEL: Forget it.

KAT: With Emily I mean, after school, so you can … we can take Baggie. Yes, I will come with you.

RACHEL: Good. Sorry. I'm supposed to be helping *you*, now you're back. Here, pass me those ones.

> *They finish loading up the baking tray and put in oven.* KAT *checks the oven controls.*

Kat. Do you reckon, if it's going to be just you and Em … that you might look after *me* in my old age?

KAT: Come on, Mum. You're not going to get it, and besides that's years away.

RACHEL: I'm just asking, 'cause you know, it's good to plan for the future …

> KAT *busies herself tidying up.*

KAT: I don't know where I'll be … or who I'll be with … surely Dad … as your friend can at least …

RACHEL: He never excelled at caring for anyone. Maybe my fault 'cause I was so good at doing everything.

KAT: Look, I'm not going to promise *not* to put you in a home, if that's why …

RACHEL: Right. Unlike lying to Nanna.

EMILY *is at the cupboard.*

KAT: You're the one who sold Gran's property, remember, even though Baggie Nanna specifically … Emily. What are you doing?

EMILY: Can I've a snack?

RACHEL: Hey, that was to help Mum get a larger house here, and to help provide for us, and you too if I recall.

KAT: But we all wanted to keep Gran's beach house, Mum. Bag Nan wanted it. Em would have loved it. [*To* EMILY] There's a treat after dinner if you can please wait …

RACHEL: What, so thanks to me your daughter misses out on a beach life, while I have a nice house and your Nanna has savings to pay for her full-time care like it's a bad thing?!

KAT: Doesn't the government pay for that?

RACHEL: What planet are you from, Kat?

EMILY: Please? I promise to eat all my dinner …

RACHEL: Look. It's not that I'm worried …

KAT: Good. [*To* EMILY] No.

EMILY *sulks back to her dolls.*

RACHEL: It's just that you've seen Bag Nan twice since coming home, and well, Emily deserves to have a relationship with her great grandmother, and ya know, I also hope to see her when she's all grown up, in case, you know, when I'm old …

KAT: Mum. Really? Bag Nan's only gotten dementia in her eighties.

RACHEL: That we know of!

KAT: Can we please stop micro-managing every future fear!

RACHEL: Says the lady who wants to ship her off to a home!

KAT: I'm not … Jeez. Well … maybe somebody has to. To help *you*.

Beat.

How much time has passed already?

RACHEL: Huh?

KAT: I mean, did we set the alarm on the oven?

RACHEL *rolls her eyes and goes to check her mobile.*

Shit. What time is it now?

> KAT *starts pressing buttons on the oven*

I don't know how to work this … stupid Air BnB …

RACHEL: Here.

> RACHEL *assists.*

I told you, you can stay at my place.

KAT: Look, I will spend time with her, okay?! It's just … crazy weird being back … and now Emily's starting proper school … and I'm trying to organise when we're going back, and I don't think I'm ready to work yet, even though I'm broke … and God, I don't even have my licence yet!

RACHEL: Right. Okay, I get it.

KAT: And besides. [*Leaning in, hoping Emily can't hear*] Last week we went to see Bag Nan, and she kept calling Emily a cat, trying to pat her and pick her up! It really bothered Emily. She kept asking me if Baggie Nan was going mad? How do I answer that?

> EMILY *has clearly heard and watches both* KAT *and* RACHEL.

RACHEL: Oh. That's odd … Why's the milk in the cupboard?

KAT: Don't look at *me*.

RACHEL: Well, It's *your* cupboard … [*Attempting a joke*] It's not long-life!

KAT: [*to* EMILY] Emily, did *you* put the milk in the cupboard?

EMILY: [*shaking her head*] Dolly? [*To Dolly*] Speak up. Use your words.

> *Doubting herself,* RACHEL *begins to retrace her own steps, mumbling to herself.* EMILY *and* KAT *watch her with concern.* RACHEL *pauses realising she's being watched.*

KAT: Mum. Now you're being paranoid. We were talking, and you had other things on your mind …

RACHEL: Yeah, no. *That* I would've remembered …

KAT: Mum, stop pretending to be …

EMILY: Is Rache Nan going mad like Baggie Nanna?

> RACHEL *pretends she doesn't hear and busies herself, cleaning up.* KAT *gives* EMILY *a stern look.*

Actually, Rache Nan. Dolly said she put the milk in the cupboard.

RACHEL: Ooh is that the time. I gotta go … check on Mum, anyway.

RACHEL *exits.*

The oven alarm goes off. KAT *rushes over to try to turn it off but can't.*

KAT: Shit …

EMILY *covers her ears and watches her mum struggle.*

SCENE TEN: 'NOT A THIEF'

Pet shop.

MAGGIE *walks into the pet shop. She stands staring at* SHOP ASSISTANT *who is on the phone. Gathering the courage,* MAGGIE *walks towards the counter to talk to her.*

SHOP ASSISTANT: [*into the phone*] … You're welcome and thank you for choosing Paula's Pets.

SHOP ASSISTANT *hangs up, then gives her attention to* MAGGIE.

Hello. How can I help you today?

MAGGIE: Hello. You might know me.

SHOP ASSISTANT: Oh, yes. I remember you. Magpie, right?

MAGGIE: Magg-ee. I have something I want to tell you. I am not a thief. I did not mean to or try to steal your husband. I didn't know he was married. I mean … You just weren't really working hard enough to keep him were you.

SHOP ASSISTANT: Ah … I might just get my supervisor.

SHOP ASSISTANT *catches the eye of the* SUPERVISOR *and waves them over.*

MAGGIE: I'm not saying it's your fault. In fact. I came here to say sorry.

SUPERVISOR *wanders over and joins them.*

SUPERVISOR: Hello. Can we help you with anything today, Mam?

MAGGIE: [*ignoring* SUPERVISOR] Because I am. I am truly sorry. But I did love him. Maybe I've taught him how to love again too. I guess you can't keep love locked in a cage.

MAGGIE *shares this fact with the audience.*

SUPERVISOR: Can we call someone for you, dear?

MAGGIE: [*to* SHOP ASSISTANT] Yes. Tell him, I still love him. But he needs to be free, so he can love again. He'll understand.

> MAGGIE *shares her cleverness and bravery with the audience. She smiles at the* SUPERVISOR *and* SHOP ASSISTANT, *who look at each other, unsure what to say or do.*

> MAGGIE *begins to walk out, but grabs a packet of birdseed and walks off with it under her arm.*

> SHOP ASSISTANT *goes to stop her for stealing, but the* SUPERVISOR *reassures* SHOP ASSISTANT *to leave it be. They watch* MAGGIE *leave.*

SCENE ELEVEN A: 'KINDNESS OF STRANGERS'

Maggie's apartment.

MAGGIE *and* INGRID *sit humming a tune together.* MAGGIE *sucks on a red icy pole that makes her lips red.*

RACHEL *hurriedly knocks on* MAGGIE*'s door, then opens door with her own set of keys and enters.*

RACHEL: It's only me, Mum. Hi.

MAGGIE: There you are! Finally.

RACHEL: Hi, Mum. You okay? [*To* INGRID] Thank you so much!

INGRID: That's okay.

RACHEL: Ingrid, right?

INGRID: Yes. You must be Rachel.

RACHEL: Nice to meet you. I'm sorry …

INGRID: Your mum is lovely. We've just been chatting about her writing.

> MAGGIE *wanders over to her bookcase and starts looking through her collection. She looks at each one closely, shares with the audience, then discards to the floor and retrieves another,, etc.*

MAGGIE: I've been trying to find one of my early publications so I can give … um … Sorry what was your name again dear?

INGRID: Ingrid.

RACHEL: Mum …

INGRID: Ah … that's okay … you don't have to …

RACHEL: Sorry about all this.

MAGGIE *continues to discard unwanted books to the floor.*

So where was she exactly?

INGRID: Just down by the lake. It was probably about two hours ago, now.

RACHEL: Yeah, sorry. I hadn't been looking at my phone. I can't believe you found me via Facebook!

MAGGIE: Here it is!

RACHEL: That's a cooking book, Mum. [*To* INGRID] She's tired. I should probably get her ready for bed. Thanks again. I can't thank you enough. Really.

INGRID: Okay sure. [*To* MAGGIE] Bye, Birdie! Was lovely to meet you.

MAGGIE: Bye. Come visit again, Kat darling.

RACHEL *shows* INGRID *out the door.*

RACHEL: Thanks again. So much.

INGRID *exits.*

You didn't use your personal alarm, Mum?

MAGGIE: Oh, no that's only in case of emergencies.

Beat.

RACHEL: Why did you leave after the dinner carer had gone? It's almost midnight! Are you hungry?

MAGGIE: I went to go to the shops, but they were closed.

RACHEL: Yeah, that's 'cause it's late, Mum. Everyone's in bed.

MAGGIE: But it's early. I'm not tired. [*Sharing with the audience*] You're not in bed.

RACHEL: Well, I was. It's dark outside. Look. Maybe that's why you got lost. Come on let's get you in your nightie.

MAGGIE: I can do that myself, thank you.

MAGGIE *shares embarrassment with the audience.*

RACHEL: I'm just trying to help.

MAGGIE: [*to* RACHEL] Stop microscoping me. Why's this jacket wet?

RACHEL: You're wearing a winter jacket and it's still twenty-five degrees out there …

MAGGIE: Pish posh. Ooh it's all wet …

RACHEL *tries to help* MAGGIE *remove her scarf, and jacket. There is a 'lazzi' of removing clothes in a tangle.*

RACHEL: Mum, what's this bruise from?

MAGGIE: Oh, I fell in the lake.

RACHEL: *In* the lake? Do you mean *next* to the lake?

MAGGIE: It's not too late. There's still time. I'm going to finish this book before morning. You'll see. It'll be my best work yet! Now I have a deadline so please leave.

RACHEL *finally removes the jacket, as* MAGGIE *walks off to her bedroom.* MAGGIE *retrieves her nightie and begins to put it over the top of her clothes.* RACHEL *tries to assist. They get a bit tangled in clothes, until* RACHEL *gives up.*

RACHEL: Okay. So you're fine to get to bed on your own, then? And … no supper? Maybe a water?

MAGGIE: Oh, stop worrying. You stay up too late. I'm … off to bed. Goodnight.

MAGGIE *lies down on her bed, half undressed, falls almost instantly asleep.*

RACHEL *takes off* MAGGIE*'s shoes. She covers* MAGGIE *tenderly with a sheet and blanket.*

RACHEL: Goodnight, Mum. I'll check on you first thing in the morning, okay? Mum. You alright?

MAGGIE *snores loudly.* RACHEL *turns some of the lights out and slowly leaves.*

SCENE ELEVEN B: 'NIGHT BEARS'

Maggie's apartment.

MAGGIE *suddenly sits up wide awake.*

MAGGIE: [*calling out in the dark*] Who's there?

ANGELA *appears out of the darkness.*

Is that you Kat? Go on back to your room. No need to be afraid.

ANGELA *stands close to* MAGGIE.

Did you have another night-bear? Mummy will be home soon.

ANGELA *sits on the edge of* MAGGIE*'s bed.*

Baggie Nanna has already read you a story, darling.

Beat.

MAGGIE *looks at the audience, sharing with them.*

[*Surrendering*] Okay, just one more, then straight back to sleep, okay?

MAGGIE *yawns and lies back down.*

ANGELA *tucks* MAGGIE *in.*

Goodnight Mummy.

ACT TWO

SCENE TWELVE: 'GET OUT'

A drive-through.

All three performers are on stage sitting, lit in isolation. RACHEL *sits centre. They talk to the other characters and look at them as if there was someone on stage next to them.*

The actors play RACHEL *during different times of her life.*

RACHEL 1 *is waiting at a Covid-test drive-through.*

RACHEL 2 *is ordering tickets at drive-in movie with her date.*

RACHEL 3 *is in her car, breaking up with her husband Dave.*

VOICEOVER: Name please?

RACHELS 1 *and* 3: It's Rachel.

RACHELS 1 *and* 2: Rache. I prefer just Rache.

VOICEOVER: Surname.

RACHEL 1: Rosenberg. Um ah … Williams. Sorry. Yes. Surname …

RACHEL 3: Can I at least keep your surname? Actually no. Jeez. Why does the woman have to … But Kat keeps your name, right?

VOICEOVER: Ms Williams.

RACHELS: Yes.

VOICEOVER: Can you confirm this is your current address?

RACHEL 1: Huh? Oh, my current …

> *Pause.*

VOICEOVER: Ms Williams.

RACHEL 1: Yes. Williams. First half of my life I was Williams. I think it has a better ring to it.

RACHEL 3: Ring? You want the ring back? I don't believe this. Go and live your own life then. Go play happy husband … After all these years you're just going to start again? At your age. Is she younger? Is she pregnant?

> *She sighs towards the audience.*

Are you going to be there for the birth?

VOICEOVER: Date of birth?

> *Beat.*

Ms Williams?

RACHEL 2: Miss Williams … but it could be Rosenberg … Mrs …

> *She flirts with imaginary passenger, a young Dave. They giggle.*

Hey, thanks for letting me pick the date. I've never actually been to a drive-in. Well not legitimately where you can actually see the movie up close and hear it too! [*Out of the window*] Hi. Can I have two tickets please? Thanks. And two choc tops. Ta. Can we park anywhere? [*Back to imaginary passenger*] Dave! I don't mean 'park' …

> *She mimes passing tickets and snacks to 'Dave' so she can drive.*

Here. Hold it.

RACHELS 1 *and* 3: Hold it!

> *They both hold up their hands over their mouths.*

RACHEL 1: Hold on. I just need a moment …

VOICEOVER: Ms Williams. If you're not able to cooperate, I'm going to have to ask …

RACHEL 2: *Ask* me. Ya have to *ask* me first before you stick your tongue down my throat, will ya! Jeez, Dave. Oh. Sshh. The movie's beginning.

RACHEL 3: At the beginning. Did she ask you or did you ask her? Was it magic like us? Or thrilling just because it was something you weren't supposed to do.

> *Beat.*

Ya know, don't answer that. Just … go … live your new life.

> *Beat.*

Get out!

RACHEL 1: Get it out! Ouch that nostril really hurt. I thought it wasn't supposed to hurt that much? Jeez!

> *She shares with the audience briefly.*

VOICEOVER: Yep. Sorry. Least it's over. You can go now.

RACHEL 1: It's over. Go now. Just go.

Beat.

Get out.

RACHEL 1 *and* RACHEL 3: Get the fuck out of my car!

> RACHEL 2 *and* RACHEL *3 stays in their moments.*

> RACHEL 1 *looks about and notices there's no-one in her car. Then she sees the Covid-tester has left.* RACHEL 1 *goes to drive but is suddenly unsure what to do next. She breathes.*

RACHEL 1: [*to herself*] Go.

> *She checks prepares to drive off.*

It's over.

SCENE THIRTEEN: 'LIE BACK AND RELAX'

Dentist's surgery.

RACHEL *and* MAGGIE *are sitting in a waiting room. A* DENTAL NURSE *wearing a face mask and shield takes their temperatures on their foreheads.* MAGGIE *is concentrating on being very still, holding her breath.*

RACHEL: Hold still for the nurse, Mum.

DENTAL NURSE: All done. Won't be long.

> MAGGIE *gasps and breathes in relief.* DENTAL NURSE *smiles and exits.*

RACHEL: Thanks.

MAGGIE: [*sharing with the audience*] Well, thank God that's over.

> MAGGIE *goes to leave.*

RACHEL: Mum, that was just the, the uh … the … temperature check.

MAGGIE: I don't have a temperature. You used to get scary temperatures. I remember when you we had to wait to have your plaster off your leg.

RACHEL: That was me with Kat.

MAGGIE: And you asked me do they melt it off or cut it off. [*Sharing with the audience*] Aww, you were so scared, Kat.

RACHEL: I'm Rachel, Mum.

MAGGIE: How's your leg now? Is that why we're here?

RACHEL: We're at the dentist. Your dentist.

MAGGIE: [*looking around*] No, I've never been here before.

> RACHEL *checks her phone and shakes her head, mumbling to herself.*

RACHEL: Mum, shall we ring Paul while we're waiting? Your son?

MAGGIE: Who?

> DENTAL NURSE *re-enters*

DENTAL NURSE: We're ready for you now, Mrs Williams.

MAGGIE: Oh no thanks. My daughter's the one with the … the um … leg …

RACHEL: [*to* DENTAL NURSE] Can I come in with her too, please?

DENTAL NURSE: Well, we're not really letting extra people in the room due to the new Covid-safety restrictions, except for children … but …

> MAGGIE *is blowing raspberries.*

We can make an exception.

RACHEL: Thank you.

> RACHEL *stands up and puts her hand out for* MAGGIE.

Come on, Mum.

> MAGGIE *doesn't move. She looks at audience then at* RACHEL*'s outstretched hand. The* DENTAL NURSE *waits patiently.*

RACHEL: Come on. The um … ah … dentist, the dentist does all the work, Mum.

> MAGGIE *shakes her head, crosses her arms and sulks.*

You don't have to do anything. You just lie back, relax, with your mouth open. Wouldn't that be nice if people did things for you, and you didn't have to worry anymore? You know like Kat says … ?

> MAGGIE *opens her mouth wide.* RACHEL *nods. They all wait.* MAGGIE *shares this with the audience, unsure who to please.*

RACHEL: [*singing and clapping*] 'Going to the dentist, dentist, dentist, going to the dentist, just like me'.

> MAGGIE *stands happily joining in the song.* RACHEL *and* MAGGIE *clap and sing: 'Going to the dentist, dentist, dentist … '* DENTAL NURSE *joins in.*

They all sing, dance, and clap, following the DENTAL NURSE, *who turns off into a nearby consult room.* MAGGIE *follows, but* RACHEL *is busy gathering her bag, and looking at her phone and hasn't noticed where they've gone.* RACHEL *starts looking hurriedly in doorways for* MAGGIE *and the* DENTAL NURSE. DENTAL NURSE *comes back out to find* RACHEL *and guides her in the right direction to the consult room.*

They all exit.

SCENE FOURTEEN: 'NOT THE BEACH'

Rachel's car.

RACHEL *is driving with* KAT *in the front passenger seat and* MAGGIE *in the back.* MAGGIE *is trying to escape out of her seat belt and getting tangled. She shares this discomfort and other moments with the audience throughout.*

MAGGIE: Oh. What is this stupid thing?

KAT: Nanna, you need to keep your seat belt on!

MAGGIE: It's so so scratchy.

> MAGGIE *shows audience how uncomfortable it is.*

Where are we?

RACHEL: Mum, remember we said we would both take you to the beach, but it's a few hours' drive, okay?

MAGGIE: I think you've past it.

KAT: Baggie Nanna, we have to be patient, okay?

MAGGIE: I'm not a patient.

> MAGGIE *groans.*

Oh, it's too … too long.

> *She looks out of the window.*

Oh here we are!

> MAGGIE *shares her seatbelt frustration with the audience.*

KAT: [*to* RACHEL] I don't think this is going to work.

RACHEL: Kat, can we please just …

KAT: It took hours just to get her out the door.

RACHEL: But this might be our last chance.

KAT: We don't know that. There are people who take them in buses to places …

RACHEL: We only need twenty minutes on the actual beach. Ten even.

MAGGIE *finds entertainment turning her head between* KAT *and* RACHEL*'s conversation.*

KAT: But it's almost twelve now.

KAT: Mum, I have to be back before six to pick Emily up.

MAGGIE: [*counting*] Six, ten, eleven, twelve … Is that Lake George?

KAT: And we're probably going to have to stop halfway …

RACHEL: Okay. Alright.

KAT: Sorry.

RACHEL: Okay. Okay! You're right, as usual.

Not the best place to try and pull over …

They pull over.

KAT: Sorry Mum.

RACHEL: Just wait till I can turn around.

Both KAT *and* RACHEL *watch for traffic.*

MAGGIE: Oh, good we're here. Not much of a swell.

KAT: Baggie Nanna. I don't think we can go to the beach today.

RACHEL: Sorry, Mum. But we can go another day, okay?

MAGGIE: Yes, I know. Those fires. But the air seems good here.

KAT: And we should probably stay in the ACT …

RACHEL: You can't trick her. I mean would you trick me if I … ?

KAT: They're suggesting people stay at home 'cause of the virus.

MAGGIE: You two just think I'm old and stupid.

RACHEL: Mum …

MAGGIE: Dementia's not contagious ya know!

KAT: [*to* RACHEL] Mum … can we just go back …

RACHEL *is still waiting for a safe time to turn around.* KAT *is trying to get reception on her phone.* MAGGIE *has undone her seatbelt.*

MAGGIE: Don't worry, I'll take myself to the beach. Tide's out, but I can walk.

MAGGIE *suddenly gets out of the car, walking almost directly into traffic.*

Cars honk as they pass by quickly.

RACHEL: Mum! Jesus! Mum!!

RACHEL *swiftly gets out of the car and takes off after* MAGGIE.

KAT *is left on her own in the passenger seat, trying to get reception on her phone.*

KAT: Fuck.

Cars pass by quickly.

KAT *gets out of the car, keeping her eyes on her phone and on* RACHEL *and* MAGGIE, *who have disappeared into the distance.* KAT *follows them, dodging traffic.*

Fuck fuck fuck fuck fuck!!

SCENE FIFTEEN A: 'HI DAVE'

Rachel's bedroom.

RACHEL *is tucked up in bed with a glass of wine, watching TV. She looks at the phone and pauses the TV with the remote. She has another sip and reaches for the phone and dials.*

RACHEL: Hi, Dave. It's me. Oh. You've got … company. I'll be quick. Just thought I would let you know that Kat and I have decided to put Mum in a home, so … Yeah. We don't need to fight over *that* anymore.

She attempts a laugh.

It could be months, but I thought you should know.

Beat.

You know you're welcome to come back … to visit … Kat and Em are still in Canberra, so they would love that, so … You know Emily is growing up so quickly. She reminds me so much of our Kat when she was little. Do you remember that time she … Oh. That's … okay. Yeah, I understand. Okay … It's just all been a bit surreal, so I guess I needed someone to tell …

She attempts a laugh.

I'm fine I just … oh you gotta go … ? Well, don't forget next Saturday …

> *'Dave' has hung up swiftly before she can finish. She returns the phone to its receiver*

Okay, then … bye. Cheers

> *She sips deeply. And reaches for the remote again.*

SCENE FIFTEEN B: 'HELLO?'

Rachel's bedroom.

ANGELA *peers round the corner and watches* RACHEL. RACHEL *stops and notices her.* ANGELA *waves hello.* RACHEL *puts down the glass, gets out of bed and turns on the light, but* ANGELA *has gone.*

RACHEL: Hello?

> RACHEL *looks to where* ANGELA *was, and about her room, including under the bed. She decides to hop back in bed, a little disturbed.*

[*Reassuring herself*] I must be tired.

SCENE SIXTEEN: 'LEAVING HOME'

Maggie's apartment.

RACHEL *is gathering clothes from Maggie's wardrobe to fold and pack.* MAGGIE *watches, and when* RACHEL *turns her back,* MAGGIE *returns the same item to the wardrobe.* MAGGIE *shares her joy and frustrations openly with the audience. This 'game' goes on for a time until …*

RACHEL: Mum. Would you just let me pack.
MAGGIE: I'm not going.
RACHEL: Please.
MAGGIE: *This* is my home.
RACHEL: Think of it as a holiday.

> MAGGIE *looks to the audience for an explanation.*

MAGGIE: [*to the audience*] Holiday?
RACHEL: [*cheerily*] Yes. Holiday. [*Under her breath*] I could do with a bloody holiday …

> RACHEL *selects items and folds them and places them in suitcase. When she turns her back,* MAGGIE *again unfolds items, returning them.* RACHEL *refuses to oblige this 'game' and continues to retrieve and pack items.*

Mum, please!

MAGGIE: [*having a mini tantrum*] My stuff. My stuff!

RACHEL: I'm helping you with your stuff.

MAGGIE: No! I'm not going! You can't make me!

RACHEL: [*getting frustrated*] Will you just let me get you ready for your … your holiday!

> *Beat.*

Please? I need a break too, Mum.

MAGGIE: Oh, okay dear. If you need a break.

> MAGGIE *wanders over to a nearby table and sits down. Satisfied,* RACHEL *keeps packing.* MAGGIE *looks at the things on the table and picks up an iPad. She picks up a texta and looks at it. Then she opens the cover of the iPad. She starts writing on the iPad's surface with texta.* RACHEL *is concentrating on closing the suitcase.*

Who shall I make it out to?

RACHEL: Huh? [*Seeing the iPad being defiled*] Mum!!

> RACHEL *rushes over to* MAGGIE *and grabs the iPad off her.*

That's my iPad!! … so we can FaceTime in case we go into lockdown again.

> RACHEL *tries to clean the iPad.*

> MAGGIE *goes over to the suitcase, closes it and sets it on the ground on its wheels.*

MAGGIE: Well, looks like you're all packed. See you when you're back from your … lockdown.

RACHEL: Mum … [*Gently*] You're the one going.

> *Beat.*

MAGGIE: Let's go then!

> MAGGIE *heads happily to the door, wheeling her own suitcase.*

RACHEL: [*tears welling up*] Thanks, Mum.

RACHEL *grabs some extra bags and tries to leave with* MAGGIE *out through the door.*

Okay. Let's go …

MAGGIE: To the beach!

RACHEL: Mum. Just … say bye to your apartment.

MAGGIE: Bye to your apartment.

MAGGIE *wheels her luggage and wanders in the wrong direction while waving at audience.*

RACHEL: This way, Mum …

MAGGIE *notices she has gone the wrong way. She shares this with the audience, then changes direction and follows* RACHEL.

They exit.

SCENE SEVENTEEN: 'DRIVING LESSON'

Rachel's car.

RACHEL *is in the passenger seat and* KAT *is behind the wheel, having a driving lesson. They are stationary in a car park.*

KAT: I'm not nervous.

RACHEL: You'll be fine. It's just a car park.

KAT: I know … Right … I can't believe I kept putting this off for so long. It's so embarrassing, in my twenties maybe, but thirty-five! Uncle Paul learned to drive when he was like sixteen or seventeen, didn't he?

RACHEL: Hey, there's literally no-one around.

KAT: You know what I mean.

RACHEL: Well, you've had a lot on your plate the last … At least it's an automatic. Jeez, when Mum taught me to drive! Oh, what, a nightmare that was!

KAT: Mum, not helping!

RACHEL: Okay, okay. Seatbelt. Check your mirrors. You're in the park …

KAT: You mean 'in park'.

RACHEL: In park, yeah, yeah …

Pause.

KAT: So, shall I turn her on?

Pause.

Mum?

RACHEL: Sorry? Where were we?

RACHEL looks about her.

Oh wait! Sorry. I'm on the wrong side.

RACHEL reaches for the steering wheel which isn't there. She is momentarily confused.

That's weird. Come on swap places.

KAT: Mum, you're giving me a driving lesson, remember?

Beat.

RACHEL: Yes … I … um …

KAT: Remember?

RACHEL: Stop asking me if I remember! I was just joking, 'cause you were nervous … trying to … lighten the mood.

KAT: You sure you're okay?

RACHEL: Of course I'm okay. Hey. No more procrastinating, alright?

KAT: [*unsure*] Okay.

RACHEL: Right.

Beat.

Okay. Engine on. In reverse. And indicate before you pull out, slowly …

SCENE EIGHTEEN A: 'ROOM WITH A VIEW'

Dementia ward.

RACHEL, *wearing a mask, walks into Maggie's new room curiously, laden with bags and carrying some items in a box.*

MAGGIE *is sitting on the bed, looking cross.*

RACHEL: Here you are! Your new room! It's … it's nice. We're lucky this room came up.

Beat.

Now. I can bring more of your things later, ya know to make it more … homey … homely … homie … cosy …

MAGGIE: No, we can't stay here!

RACHEL *gives a huge sigh.*

RACHEL: Why not?

MAGGIE *shares a sigh with the audience about how stupid this question is.*

MAGGIE: Well, it's down. Downstairs. I wouldn't feel safe. There's no balcony.

RACHEL *starts to put items down or place them in the room, hanging up clothes, etc.*

We've always had a balcony, Remember? To BBQ our our our … crawly porns. I can't even see the bay from here! You have to go ask for an upstairs room. It's safer.

RACHEL: Mum, we're not down the coast, we're still in Canberra …

MAGGIE: And where are *you* going to sleep? I'm not going head-to-toe in that!

MAGGIE *shares with the audience how ridiculous the situation is.*

RACHEL: Mum …

CARER *knocks and enters.*

CARER: Hello! Welcome. You must be Margaret. I've heard heaps about you. I'm Lanie. Are we enjoying our new room?

MAGGIE: Can we please explain to my daughter that we need a double twin upstairs with a view. We've always had a double view.

RACHEL: Excuse me. Sorry. I'll just get the rest of the things from the car.

RACHEL *leaves.*

CARER: Why don't we start by washing hands together? This is your sink. Here's the water. Here's the soap dispenser. Yes, that's right.

CARER *and* MAGGIE *mime washing hands.*

[*Singing*] 'Happy Birthday to you.'

MAGGIE *joins in singing along.*

MAGGIE *and* CARER: 'Happy Birthday to you. Happy Birthday dear … Maggie. Happy Birthday to you.'

MAGGIE: Hip hip …

CARER: Rinse …

> *She rinses.*

MAGGIE: Hooray!

CARER: And pat dry over here on this paper towel …

> *They do it together.*

MAGGIE *and* CARER: Hooray!

MAGGIE: Hip hip …

CARER: And in the bin …

> *They put it in the bin.*

MAGGIE *and* CARER: Hooray!!

CARER: All done.

> ANGELA *enters and watches them.*

MAGGIE: [*to* ANGELA] It's my birthday today. I'm thirty-one. [*To* CARER] Am I thirty-one?

CARER: Eighty-one I heard. I'll be back in a minute, okay?

> CARER *leaves.* MAGGIE *looks at audience as if in disbelief, then looks around room.*

> ANGELA *stays and watches* MAGGIE.

SCENE EIGHTEEN B: 'SILLY KAT'

Dementia ward.

MAGGIE: [*to* ANGELA] Oh hello, there! I'm so glad you came to see me for my birthday! Come in and give your Grand Baggie Nanna a big birthday hug!

> ANGELA *opens her arms as she walks towards* MAGGIE. MAGGIE *hugs* ANGELA.

Where's your mum?

> ANGELA *points to towards the hallway.*

Out there? Tell her to come in.

> ANGELA *walks back out into the hall.*

Emily? Where you going? Go get Kat.

CARER *returns with a box of books and a couple of items.*

CARER: Back again. Your daughter had to go. She left you these, and said she'd visit you soon.

MAGGIE: Kat, you finally visited me. You shouldn't let Emily wander about …

She goes to hug CARER *and pauses.*

Oh … you're …

CARER: I'm Lanie, darling, one of your carers.

MAGGIE *looks in the hallway for* ANGELA.

MAGGIE: Kat? Kitty Kat?

CARER: Ooh, I don't think there's a cat there, dear …

MAGGIE: No. My Kat.

CARER: Did you used to have a cat? We have a therapy dog that visits.

MAGGIE: No, no, my granddaughter. Her Emily's out there on her own.

MAGGIE *is still looking down the corridor.*

Silly Kat. Always irresponsible.

CARER: They'll be in sooner or later. Come on, let's get you unpacked. We're having chicken for dinner with gravy. Your daughter tells me you like gravy, but no peas.

MAGGIE: No peas. I'm not wearing peas.

CARER: No peas. Got it.

They start unpacking together.

SCENE NINETEEN: 'RUMMAGE'

Maggie's apartment.

RACHEL *and* MAGGIE *go through various items in Maggie's old apartment. There are boxes everywhere and a pile of bedding and clothes on the floor.* EMILY *sits reading some of Maggie's books.*

RACHEL: Oh Kat, do you remember this?

RACHEL *holds up an old dress.*

It was Gran's, my gran. Maggie's mum's. Her wedding dress!

KAT: It's all ripped.

RACHEL: It's like from the … the twenties!

EMILY: Ooh, can I try it on, Rache Nan?!

KAT: Darling it's way too big and probably really old and smelly.

> *Beat.*

EMILY: What's this?!

> EMILY *is holding a bright pink glittery dildo.* KAT *lets out an uncontrolled audible sound and* RACHEL *laughs loudly, snorting.*

Can I have it?

KAT *and* RACHEL: No!

> KAT *swiftly grabs the vibrator from* EMILY *and puts it in the bin.*

KAT: Let's see what we can find here … Look! Isn't *this* pretty …

> KAT *grabs the nearest item and hands it to* EMILY *to distract her from the dildo in the bin.* KAT *continues looking at bric-a-brac.*

Do you want any of these, Mum?

EMILY: Ooh a tea set!

RACHEL: Oh my God, I remember these. Gran and Mum were always using these. We used to have the strongest tea from the pot with leaves and all, and like three sugars in these tiny cups!

EMILY: Can I play with it, Mum?

KAT: Be careful

RACHEL: [*to* EMILY] It's got actual gold on it. Look!

EMILY: Wow. Gold? Are we rich?

> EMILY *lifts her little finger daintily and sips from the cup and saucer.*

KAT: I wouldn't put your mouth to it, Em. It's probably filthy.

> EMILY *is excited and starts setting out the tea set as* KAT *watches. Deeper in the box* RACHEL *makes a new discovery.*

RACHEL: Oh, wow look at this!

> RACHEL *pulls out an old box full of circus things. There is a framed old circus picture of Maggie, a scrap book of newspaper cuttings, some very old dried-up clown make-up, wig, neck ruff, skirt, balls, fake flowers, scarves and a red nose.* EMILY *is fascinated by each item.*

Wow. Oh, I remember seeing this!

> RACHEL *opens a scrap book and looks at an old newspaper cutting of Maggie on a trapeze.* KAT *comes over and looks on.* EMILY *puts on the red nose and continues to look at and play with other items that are now strewn about.*

KAT *and* RACHEL: [*reading together*] 'Birdie flies high.'

KAT: That outfit! Woohoo Nanna! It looks like a seventies drag outfit.

RACHEL: What a huge circus tent. And look.

> RACHEL *dusts off the picture frame.* EMILY *comes over to look too, still wearing the red nose.*

This one's in colour. Wow. Mum … as a clown. Gosh she was so young.

KAT: She's actually quite cute in this pic. That make-up though. And fake lashes back then?

RACHEL: She was beautiful.

EMILY: She looks sad.

> *Beat.*

EMILY: Oh! Are these juggling balls?

> EMILY *grabs the balls and attempts to juggle. Balls are randomly tossed left and right and retrieved by* EMILY *throughout the following several lines of text.*

RACHEL: This feels … wrong.

KAT: How else are we going to decide what we keep and what we don't.

RACHEL: I just wish we were doing this *with* Baggie Nanna. She has so many memories here.

KAT: How come we never saw any of these, even after packing up Gran's beach house? You could have at least showed us. Emily and I would have loved to have seen these? [*To* EMILY] Careful, darling.

RACHEL: We did, actually. Baggie and I showed you and Emily when she was like two, one time you visited. I remember you kept saying she was too young. And anyway, you were always off busy doing things when we played with Emily, so …

KAT: Oh, so that's my fault she missed out. That I miss out. You never tell me things, Mum. Like keeping me in the dark about Dad!

A juggling ball hits something.

[*To* EMILY] Emily!!

KAT: / I can't believe you kicked Dad out. You should be lucky he's still alive!

RACHEL: / Will you stop blaming me for things not working out for you.

Silence.

Kat …

KAT: Sorry …

RACHEL: Before. I meant … it feels wrong … all of it. Just going through her stuff like, like she's … dead.

KAT: Don't you think I don't know that?! Look. [*Almost whispering*] I don't want to upset Emily. She's the one in the middle of all this …

EMILY *is happily playing dress-ups with all the clown items, including the red nose.*

RACHEL: It's just we never even asked her. Mum. For her permission.

KAT: Mum. You've done such a good job with her over the years. God. I recall she didn't listen to you when she could anyway. Let's just … let it go.

EMILY *makes funny faces while watching* KAT *and* RACHEL.

Beat.

RACHEL: Are you going to at least ask *me*?

KAT: What? Oh, Mum …

RACHEL: When you think I can't choose or do things for myself?

KAT: I'm not doing this now.

RACHEL: Then when Kat?!

KAT: We've got years before this …

RACHEL: How do you know that?

RACHEL *starts crying.*

You of all people should know that's not true!

EMILY: What's wrong with Rache Nan? [*In a silly voice*] Is she demented too, now?

RACHEL: Emily!

KAT: / Rache. Of course you're not …

RACHEL: / I just need some … um … air.

I'm late to check on … I mean visit Mum.

RACHEL *grabs her handbag and heads swiftly for the door.*

KAT: Shit.

KAT *suddenly looks at* EMILY, *who's been throwing a scarf in the air and now stands with her mouth wide open with enjoyed disgust at her mother's swearing.*

SCENE TWENTY: 'LOST GIRL'

Shopping mall.

Shopping mall background sounds.

RACHEL *is sitting down at the mall. She is rummaging through her handbag, emptying the contents and replacing them as if she has lost something. She looks around, unsure. A* GIRL *stands watching her.*

RACHEL: Hello. Are you lost?

GIRL: No. Are *you* lost?

RACHEL: That's a funny thing to ask. Grown-ups don't get lost. I can help you, if you like …

GIRL: I'm not supposed to talk to people I haven't met.

RACHEL: Well, my name is Rachel. I'm a teacher.

GIRL: I'm going to swimming lessons.

RACHEL: Ooh, at the beach?

The GIRL *looks at* RACHEL *oddly.*

GIRL: My mummy's taking me to the pool.

RACHEL: And where's your mummy?

GIRL: Where's *YOUR* mummy?

RACHEL: Well, she's …

RACHEL *pauses, stumped by this question. She looks about, then she sees the* GIRL *again, stands and gathers her shopping.*

Oh, there you are, Kitty Kat. Come on.

GIRL: I'm not a cat.

RACHEL: We better not miss Gran's, um, Baggie Nan's chicken dinner! Come on …

RACHEL *suddenly takes hold of* GIRL*'s hand and goes to leave with her.* GIRL *screams and pulls away*

GIRL: Let go, you crazy woman!

RACHEL: [*letting go*] Sorry. I thought …

GIRL: Mum!!

GIRL *runs off.*

RACHEL: I'm sorry. Sorry …

RACHEL *looks about, shaken and exits.* RACHEL *re-enters, grabs her forgotten shopping, trying to hide her embarrassment as she again exits.*

ACT THREE

All three performers stand, lit in isolation. KAT *is centre. They talk to the other characters and look at them as if there was someone there.*

The actors play KAT *during different times of her life, standing in front of or talking through a door.*

KAT 1 *stands outside the bathroom door talking to her mum, who is inside.*

KAT 2 *hides inside the bathroom, waiting for pregnancy test results, talking to her boyfriend Sammy, who is outside.*

KAT 3 *stands outside her front door, letting down a potential date.*

There is a knock at the door.

ALL KATS: One minute!

KAT 1: [*knocking*] I'm waiting one more minute! You're not supposed to lock it. It's only me. Are you trying on your new swimmers now?

> *Beat.*

Are you doing a poo?

> *Beat.*

Hey do you have the iPad in there? I've packed everything but can't find it. We're gunna run out of time. I'm not kidding

> *Pause.*

Can you hear me?

KAT 2: Yeah! I can hear you! Hang on a minute will ya …

> *She looks at her watch.*

We're not late.

> KAT *has just done a home-kit pregnancy test. She places it on the bathroom sink ledge. She looks in the bathroom mirror.*

[*To herself*] *I'm* just late.

> KAT 1 *knocks on the door.*

[*Shouting through the door*] Hey, beauty doesn't happen in seconds you know … [*To herself, looking at the test*] Second stripe …

> *She holds the pregnancy test and looks at it more closely, and at the instructions, her watch, then back at the test stick.*

> KAT 1 *knocks on the door.*

[*Shouting*] Oh, go wee outside!

> KAT 2 *looks at the pregnancy test absorbing the results.*

[*To herself*] Two stripes.

> KAT 2 *looks into the bathroom mirror talking to herself.*

Well, Kat. We better go tell him. [*Shouting*] Sammy! Guess what?

> KAT 1 *knocks on the door.*

> KAT 3 *steps outside her front door.*

KAT 3: Hi. I'm sorry I'm not ready. Oh, wow … you look … nice.

> *Pausing outside her door. She closes it gently behind her.*

About tonight. The babysitter cancelled … again, but I'm not ready anyway. I mean to date again. It's too soon for me. Sorry.

> *She goes to leave, but turns back.*

And you know what, it's Kat not Kath.

> I gotta go read a bedtime story now … It's getting late …

> *She creeps back inside.*

KAT 1: It's late. I mean it's too late to go now. Please unlock the door.

> *Pause.*

We don't have to do anything if you don't want to … but I need you to unlock the door so I can see you're okay … Please?

> Hey, let's plan a trip to the beach *next* weekend? Just the two of us, okay? I promise this time.

> *Beat.*

I bet that shop still sells our favourite ice cream.

Beat.

It's me, Kat.

Beat.

Mum? You okay?

SCENE TWENTY-TWO: 'LOCKED OUT'

Kat's apartment.

KAT *is standing outside the bathroom talking to* EMILY *who has locked herself in.* EMILY *is hugging and talking quietly to her dolly. She is wearing the red nose.*

EMILY: Stop asking me if I'm okay!

KAT: Come on, Em. Hey, you can come with me to visit Baggie Nanna or Rache Nan whenever you want, okay? I mean … no pressure.

> *Beat.*

Em?

EMILY: I hate you all. You're all old, boring, stupid, bossy, dumb, brainless, zombie grown-ups!

KAT: Darling, we've talked about this. Zombies aren't real. And it's not nice to speak to people like that.

> *Beat.*

Do you miss your friends in Sydney? We can go back soon if you like, honey?

EMILY: Go away.

> *Beat.*

KAT: Maybe you're right. We're all dumb and stupid and …

EMILY: I want Dad.

KAT: Em.

EMILY: He's fun and funny, and no-one needs to look after him, or care for him. And he never says stupid things, or cries, or tells me what to do!

> *Beat.*

KAT: I know it's hard. And you miss him sweetie. I miss him too.

> *Beat.*

He wouldn't want to see you upset and locked in the bathroom … without being able to give you a hug, would he? Em?

EMILY: Go away.

> *Beat.*

KAT: Can I give you a hug?

EMILY: No!

KAT: Just one?

> *Beat.*

What if I told you I was sad about Daddy too. And I miss him. And sometimes *I* need a hug. And if we both had a hug together, we might feel half as sad? And it might be like we're both … [*Almost to herself*] hugging him.

> KAT *sits slumped, giving up. The bathroom door opens slowly, and* EMILY *sticks her head out. She is wearing* MAGGIE*'s clown red nose. Slowly and tenderly, they hug.*

SCENE TWENTY-THREE: 'DANCING CONFESSIONS'

Dementia ward.

RACHEL *enters Maggie's room wearing a mask.* MAGGIE *isn't there.*

RACHEL: Hello?

MAGGIE: [*offstage*] I'm just in here doing a poo!

RACHEL: Oh charming. Do you want me to get a carer? I'll close the toilet door shall I, Mum?

MAGGIE: [*entering*] No need. All done.

RACHEL: Mum, your pants.

> MAGGIE *nearly trips then pulls up her pants. She shares this with the audience.*

Don't forget to wash your hands.

MAGGIE: No, no.

> I did that this morning already. Now. This TV.

> MAGGIE *shows* RACHEL *a CD player*

It's broken.

RACHEL: It's a CD player Mum. It plays music. I brought all your CDs from your apartment.

MAGGIE: Yes, I know. Your apart …

RACHEL: We just have to turn it on, like this.

Music starts playing.

There you go. Works just fine. It's from your apartment.

MAGGIE: No, the carer bought it.

RACHEL: Brought … bring brought …

MAGGIE: Bought brought ought. [*Sharing with the audience*] Shoulda coulda … ought …

RACHEL: Sure, Mum.

Beat.

MAGGIE: And friendships broken.

Beat.

No-one visits. Remember … with the trumpet husband?

RACHEL: It's because of the restrictions … the virus. Melbourne's having another … Hey, let's take a picture—we can send it to friends?

MAGGIE: What's that on your face?

RACHEL: Oh, just a mask. That's the rules …

RACHEL *tries to take a selfie, but* MAGGIE *is wondering what she's taking a picture of.*

MAGGIE: That's my phone.

RACHEL: It's *my* phone, Mum. I'm trying to take a selfie.

MAGGIE: Selfish?

MAGGIE *scoffs and shares this with the audience.*

RACHEL: Selfie. A picture of us.

MAGGIE: Where? Who's that?

MAGGIE *is squinting and straining trying to see the phone.*

RACHEL: It's us, now. Look, that's us. Hello.

RACHEL *waves at mobile camera.*

MAGGIE: No, that's not right. They're … boring. Come on, let's have a dance, for old time's sake.

RACHEL, *disappointed, puts the phone away and they stand and start to dance cheek to cheek.* RACHEL *leads.* MAGGIE *seems less stressed.* MAGGIE *hums a tune separate to the one playing on the CD player.*

RACHEL: Mum, I'm sorry I never asked you about …

Um … everything. You know all your stuff and coming here, and your apartment, it's just …

MAGGIE: [*twirling*] Apart … meant apart! You're apart, now … we're meant to …

They continue to dance slowly, and MAGGIE *takes a twirl.*

You know, darling, I know that you know.

About 'him'. I'm sorry I never told you.

RACHEL: What?

MAGGIE: Oh, I know you forgive me. But *you* should've kept dancing with me after we were married. [*Twirling*] You know, I'm not seeing him anymore, don't you, Bill.

RACHEL: Mum … ?

MAGGIE: Don't worry. Rachel is yours. But I'm leaving you.

Beat.

RACHEL: [*holding back tears*] I … I forgive you, Marg.

MAGGIE: Come on. One last dance then.

They dance

I still love you Bill, ya big oaf.

Beat.

RACHEL: [*through tears*] I love you too, Mu … Marg.

MAGGIE: And you should tell Kat.

RACHEL: About you and Dad?

MAGGIE: No, silly. About catching dementia. She'll understand.

A nearby resident yells out to turn the music down. MAGGIE *waves hand dismissively, grunting, and continues dancing.*

[*To* RACHEL] What are those people doing over there lying around, trying to sleep?

RACHEL: Mum they're really old.

MAGGIE: So? I'm old. You're old.

They stop dancing.

Why are they just lying there?

RACHEL: Maybe they're sick?

MAGGIE: Is it that virus?! In here?

MAGGIE *looks to audience in horror.*

No no no. They shouldn't be here. Get out! All of you! You can't make my baby sick!

RACHEL: It's okay. You can't catch it. They have … [*quietly*] dementia.

MAGGIE: What? Don't be silly? That's what I had, and I got better. You'll get better too, once you stop all your worrying. Always a worry wart. How's your ankle? You know you shouldn't play hide and seek up in that cupboard. You'll teach your little brother bad habits. I'm going to do a poo.

RACHEL: Mum … I gotta go.

MAGGIE *suddenly takes off down the hall.*

[*Shouting after her*] Don't forget to wash your hands!

MAGGIE: [*shouting back*] Yeah, Yeah, I know. It's my birthday.

RACHEL *watches fondly as* MAGGIE *sings happy birthday, dancing down the hall, and holding her bottom, in desperate need of the toilet.*

SCENE TWENTY-FOUR A: 'GOODBYE DAVE'

Rachel's bedroom.

RACHEL *is tucked up in bed, talking on the phone.*

RACHEL: … of course I haven't called to make you feel bad … Well, no-one can visit her anyway, 'cause the whole facility is in lockdown … Yes, I know that. Dave. You know why I … Come on, it's not that big an ask. Just sign it, scan it and send it please. I'm battling enough with all Mum's paperwork and the bank said … Yes. I did that. And now they say I have until … Can you not interrupt … what? Oh, can we not do this please … Says he who can afford the best family lawyer because you haven't had to work part time and be the mother, carer, home-maker and all the rest of it and take a massive dive in pay, while your partner just waltzes off to their career! … Whatya think it's supposed to mean? I mean just that … Ha ha. Hey, you're the one who said to me … If you. If you let me … If you would just let me finish. Just. One. time … Oh, that's funny. You're still funny … I didn't say that. I would remember … No, I am not going mad … Kat said what? Why do you have to … Oh that's … Yes. Yes, I am of sound mind. Jesus, Dave! Would you just sign the fucking … no you're the hysterical one! I'm simply. Nicely. Asking you please. For once. Just. Help me out. Then we can …

'Dave' has hung up.

Oh great. Just. Great. Grumpy old man syndrome strikes again!

RACHEL attempts to hang up the phone but it tumbles off its hook. She tries to replace it again, but misses. She bangs it several times then finally throws it across the room. She takes a breath.

Now, *that* is what we would describe as hysterical boys and girls. [*Into the phone, as if to 'Dave'*] I mean it's just as well you left. You'd just find a reason to treat me like shit anyway. [*To herself*] Grow old together my arse! [*Yelling*] Random strangers are nicer to me than you've ever been!

She settles herself, sitting up in bed under the covers and reaches for her wine.

Cheers and … go fuck yourself.

She toasts and sips deeply.

SCENE TWENTY-FOUR B: 'REMOTE'

Rachel's bedroom.

RACHEL *puts the wine glass on the bedside table and reaches for the chocolate. She stuffs a large piece in her mouth and grabs the remote. She can't seem to figure out how to use it.*

RACHEL: Oh, that's … odd … Bloody hell!

She tries some buttons.

Come on … stupid … thing …

ANGELA appears. RACHEL hands the remote to ANGELA.

Can you please show me how to … I must've grabbed the wrong one …
I don't have my glasses, or maybe it needs batteries or something.

> ANGELA *points it at the TV.* RACHEL *is pleased it works.* ANGELA
> *hands it back to* RACHEL *and exits.* RACHEL *is busy looking at*
> *the remote and how it works and the channels and doesn't notice*
> ANGELA *leave.*

Thank you very …

> RACHEL *notices* ANGELA *has gone. She looks back at the TV*
> *and stares closely at it and through to the audience. She looks at*
> *audience with the remote pointing at them in her hand.*

SCENE TWENTY-FIVE: 'NOT OFFICIAL DIAGNOSIS'

Doctor's rooms.

RACHEL: What kind of diagnosis is that? Maybe my … skull has always
looked like that? That was my first MI … MR … MRI or whatever
it's called, so how do they know? Huh?

DOCTOR: Well, it's not an official diagnosis, but it's worth considering
further tests.

RACHEL: What? But Mum was like … in her mid-seventies … maybe
it's hormones.

DOCTOR: Just to rule things out …

RACHEL: But I'm just exhausted from my job. I teach high school. And
packing up Mum's flat, the endless bloody cleaning, trying to be a
grandmother, mother, daughter. Did you know my granddaughter
can't dress herself without me?! God help her when she's a teenager
trying to do her homework, right?!

> *She forces a laugh.*

I'm just stressed having to still sort out things with my bloody ex,
and looking after Mum. You know she can barely figure out how to
get dressed! I haven't slept since … I dunno … the eighties!

> *She tries to make a joke.*

Isn't this menopause?

DOCTOR: [*writing*] I can write you a letter if you think taking time off
work is a good idea?

RACHEL *shakes her head.*

RACHEL: They can't know. Unless. Do you think teenagers can tell …

DOCTOR: So, this is a referral for a geriatric nurse. It might be a good idea to take someone with you. Maybe your partner, um your ex, or your eldest daughter? For support.

RACHEL: I … I can't. I can't tell her. Geriatric? Jeez.

DOCTOR: Look … a confirmed diagnosis is a good thing. It means we can try you on some medication straight away, so we can hopefully pause symptoms, slow things down, so you can manage things and hopefully still work and have a relatively normal life. It's proven quite effective these days … in some people.

DOCTOR *hands a referral letter to* RACHEL.

RACHEL: Some people … I've only just turned fifty-two. I mean fifty-four. God! [*Attempting a joke*] Us women get so used to lying about our age, huh?

Geriatric nurse. A nurse? Fuck. Sorry, I mean …

Beat.

Fuck.

SCENE TWENTY-SIX: 'JABBED'

Nurse's rooms.

KAT *and* EMILY *are having a flu shot.* NURSE *wears a mask.* EMILY *is wearing the red nose.*

KAT: Remember honey, the nurse says it won't hurt if you relax …

NURSE: Okay. Hold very still.

KAT: Re-laax …

NURSE: Good. And just a pinch …

EMILY: Ouch. Mum!

NURSE: And a little bit longer … Nice and still … And you're all done! There you go.

She hands EMILY *a lollipop.*

This is for you.

KAT: Well done, darling!

EMILY *rubs her arm.*

You were very brave! Say thank you to the nurse.

EMILY: [*in a very silly voice*] Thank you.

KAT: Emily. Take that thing off.

EMILY *leaves the nose on and blows a raspberry at her mum.*

Now. Mummy's turn!

NURSE: Vaccinations are very important at the moment, aren't they?

EMILY: My Great Uncle Paul doesn't believe they exist. He's an anti-vaximinator!

KAT: Well. It means he can't visit his own mother. He'll probably never see her again …

NURSE *gets the flu shot ready.* KAT *lifts her shirt to free her shoulder.*

EMILY: We can't see my great great great great great great grandmother. She's locked in a demented wand.

KAT: Dementia ward sweetie. It's actually called a Memory Support Unit.

NURSE: That sounds nice. Okay … nice and still for me …

KAT: And they're in lockdown. She's not locked up …

NURSE *gives her the flu shot.*

Shit!! I mean … ouch.

EMILY *is joyfully surprised at her mum's swearing*

EMILY: Shit shot, Mum.

KAT: Emily!

EMILY: Mummy!

KAT: Darling. Say you're sorry.

EMILY: You're sorry.

KAT: To the doctor.

NURSE: I'm a nurse.

KAT: Yes. Yeah, I meant …

EMILY: Can I have your lollipop, Mummy?

KAT*'s mobile rings, and she rummages to retrieve it.*

EMILY *grabs* KAT*'s lollipop.*

NURSE: I'll see you in reception. You'll have to wait fifteen minutes, remember?

NURSE *exits.* KAT *nods to* NURSE *as they get up to follow her out.* EMILY *is jumping about from the sugar.*

KAT: Hi, Mum. What, now? Hang on. [*To* EMILY] I'm just on the phone to Rache Nan. [*Referring to the second lollipop*] Uh-uh. Can you save that for later, please. [*Back into the phone*] Sorry Mum. Can I call you back? … Well, is it important, *now*? We'll be home in half an hour. Just at the doctors with Emily getting …

EMILY *has one of the juggling balls and begins bouncing and throwing it about.*

Emily! [*Into the phone*] I'll have to call you back.

She rubs her arm.

Well, when I get home, I just said. Yes, about half an hour or so. Well, okay. Bye.

She hangs up.

[*Yelling at* EMILY] Can we just wait quietly please? Is that too much to ask?!

EMILY *collects her ball and sits sulkily.* KAT *sits back with her eyes closed and sighs deeply.*

EMILY: [*under her breath*] Shit shot, Mum.

SCENE TWENTY-SEVEN: 'GAS AND TONIC'

Rachel's apartment.

RACHEL *is slumped on a chair facing the oven door, which is open.*

KAT *enters shouting into the phone, gagging and coughing, and covering her nose and mouth.*

KAT: Yes, that's the right address. Please hurry.

KAT *rushes to* RACHEL, *calling her name.* KAT *turns off the oven and closes the oven door. She tries to wake* RACHEL, *shouting 'Mum!'* KAT *pulls* RACHEL *from her seat to the floor and drags her out the door. They collapse on the ground outside.* RACHEL *is semi-conscious.* KAT *is coughing and calling 'Mum!'* KAT *reaches for her phone again and speaks into it.*

[*Into the phone*] … Yes, I'm still here. She's kinda conscious. Yep. We're outside now. [*To* RACHEL*, coughing*] Mum! [*Gently shaking* RACHEL] Come on. Wake up. Take some deep breaths.

RACHEL: Kitty Kat …

KAT: [*into the phone*] … She's talking a bit. [*To* RACHEL] Don't make me give you mouth to mouth. And if I have to start CPR I'm not going to hesitate to break ribs, Mum!

> KAT *half lifts* RACHEL *so that she is partially sitting and leaning on* KAT.

RACHEL: [*coming round*] No.

KAT: You okay?

RACHEL: [*drowsily , coughing*] I'm sorry, darling.

KAT: You're welcome. Jeezes. You scared me. What were you thinking … ?!

RACHEL: I can't tell you. I've left nothing behind.

KAT: [*into phone*] Yeah, she seems okay. [*To* RACHEL] You've got me.

RACHEL: You've got Emily.

KAT: Yes. And we've got you.

> KAT *puts phone aside.*

We both need you. Mum?

> RACHEL *coughs.*

Do you need a drink?

RACHEL: Gin and tonic!

KAT: I mean water. I don't think you're supposed to mix alcohol with gas.

> They both laugh at the ridiculousness of the previous statement, coughing.

> Distant ambulance sirens.

That's for you, that.

RACHEL: That's not a …

KAT: … an ambulance.

RACHEL: … gin and tonic.

> Sound of sirens getting nearer.

She was the smartest, wildest, bravest, most fun person I knew. Mum, your Baggie.

KAT: That's you, Mum. To me.
RACHEL: Oh … Darling girl.

> *Siren gets louder as ambulance approaches.*

Come on we better get up then.

> *She can't move.*

KAT: Just stay here, Mum. I'm with you.
RACHEL: I didn't mean to …

> *Beat.*

KAT: Hey, Mum.
RACHEL: Yeah?
KAT: Just so you know … if you ever do this shit again … I'll kill you!

> *They both laugh and cry together, as lights flash red and blue.*

SCENE TWENTY-EIGHT: 'SEAGULLS PLAY'

Dementia ward.

NURSE *walks into* MAGGIE*'s room to find* KAT *and* MAGGIE *playing together, making squawking sounds.*

NURSE: Just popped in to do Margaret's obs.

> MAGGIE *and* KAT *are pretending to be seagulls, flying and squawking.*

MAGGIE *and* KAT: Aahh!! Aagh!
KAT: [*to* NURSE] Oh, come in. [*To* MAGGIE] Baggie Nanna, let's pause for a bit and help the carer, ah nurse, okay?

> MAGGIE *is posing as a seagull still. She clearly understands, yet looks cheekily at audience then suddenly squawks, flaps her wings, winks at the audience and 'flies' out the room, into the hallway.* KAT *shrugs apologetically to the nurse*

NURSE: I can come back in a few minutes.

> NURSE *exits.*

> MAGGIE *and* KAT *continue their play. Together they fly around the ward and squawk loudly.* KAT *follows* MAGGIE*'s lead.* MAGGIE *pauses.* KAT *copies, still squawking.* MAGGIE *suddenly*

sits. KAT *copies, still thinking they are being sea gulls.* MAGGIE *goes rigid, and begins to have a seizure, then goes limp.*

KAT: Bag Nan? Nurse! Help. Somebody!!

SCENE TWENTY-NINE: 'PUSH TO THE PARTY'

Dementia ward.

RACHEL *wheels* MAGGIE, *who is in a wheelchair.*

MAGGIE: Oh I'm falling. Heeeelp …

RACHEL: No. Mum. It's me. I'm driving you.

MAGGIE: [*sharing with the audience*] Terrible driver!

RACHEL: Oh, thanks Mum. Such an honest relationship we have now. So … I'm signing you out today. Just for an hour …

MAGGIE: You sure?

RACHEL: Yeah. It's your birthday.

MAGGIE: [*shaking her head*] We did that already.

RACHEL: Mum. We're going to the café for your birthday. Isn't that great? We're allowed to sign you out and have a gathering with everyone! We've booked a table. And Kat and Emily will be there! And some of your writing friends! Remember Jackeline and Peta?

MAGGIE: And your Bill?

RACHEL: My *Dave* … can't make it, 'cause he's an asshole, who's moved back to Sydney, and they've got hot spots anyway, so … let's put this jacket on to keep warm, okay?

She begins dressing MAGGIE *in her jacket.*

MAGGIE: Bill used to make me happy. I thought I was going to burn up in his hotspots.

MAGGIE *tries to take off the jacket before it is on.*

RACHEL: Mum. Would you just let me. You need a jacket.

MAGGIE: Not mine. It's too heavy …

RACHEL: It's cold outside.

MAGGIE: Nonsense. Beach weather.

RACHEL: Hey, remember how we used to laugh on the most freezing frosty mornings and say 'it's beach weather' to that grumpy neighbour, the one with the fat cat?

MAGGIE: I remember, Kat.

> RACHEL *continues to dress* MAGGIE. *There is some tangle working around the wheelchair, but eventually she is wearing her jacket.*

RACHEL: Okay. Done. Phew. Let's go …

MAGGIE: You've gotta go now. Bye darling. Always busy busy busy …

RACHEL: We're both going.

MAGGIE: No, no.

RACHEL: Mum. It's your birthday.

> MAGGIE *sighs at audience as if she believes* RACHEL *doesn't understand.* RACHEL *begins pushing* MAGGIE *in her wheelchair again.*

Off to your party!!

MAGGIE: Ooh I'm falling.

RACHEL: Mum. I'm behind you.

MAGGIE: Why are you behind me. I can't see you.

RACHEL: I'm pushing you.

MAGGIE: Pushy. Pushy.

RACHEL: Yeah, funny hey?

> RACHEL *continues to push* MAGGIE *down the hallway.* MAGGIE *forgets she is being pushed by* RACHEL.

MAGGIE: Oh no I'm driving. [*Sharing her panic with the audience*] I can't stop. [*Reaching out to the audience*] Help me. Help!

RACHEL: Mum. I'm driving you.

MAGGIE: You never learned to drive!

RACHEL: That was Kat.

MAGGIE: Kat?

RACHEL: Come on. Kat's waiting …

MAGGIE: Stop stop stop! I'm falling …

RACHEL: Okay. I'll just sign you out …

> *They pause near the entrance.* RACHEL *is signing a form.* MAGGIE *is stressed and unsure where she is.*

… for your birthday. Isn't that exciting? Everyone's waiting.

> MAGGIE *looks closely at the audience trying to recognise them.*

You're eighty-three today. Paul will be there too! Your son. Paul. My brother … It's been ages …

> RACHEL *attempts to open the door whilst pushing wheelchair.*

MAGGIE: [*beginning to panic*] No no no no no. I'm twenty-nine. Twenty-nine. Twenty-nine. You can't make me! You can't put me in a home. This is intolerable! Intolerable!!

> MAGGIE *tries to get up out of the chair, almost falling out.*

RACHEL: Mum!

> MAGGIE *grabs her chest and looks as if she might have an anxiety or heart attack.* RACHEL *surrenders.*

Okay Mum. It's okay.

> RACHEL *sits down on the floor and gets out her phone.*

[*Into the phone*] Hi. It's me. We're gunna be a bit longer … Oh. Sorry I called you by accident. I meant to …

> RACHEL *suddenly hangs up.*

> LANIE, *a carer, enters and stops when she sees them both.*

LANIE: Oh, I wouldn't be sitting on the floor if I were you, Rachel …

RACHEL: Oh hi, Lanie. [*Getting up*] Yep, sorry …

LANIE: Margaret, you still here? I thought you were going out for birthday cake and ice cream?

MAGGIE: Ice cream?

> *She looks to the audience.*

Yes please! [*To* RACHEL] Come on … you. Let's go, spit spot. You drive, then.

> RACHEL *wheels a happy* MAGGIE *out through the door as* LANIE *holds it open for them.*

RACHEL: [*mouthing to* LANIE] Thank you.

MAGGIE: I scream!!

> MAGGIE *sings ice-cream van music (e.g. 'Greensleeves').* RACHEL *joins in, wheeling* MAGGIE *offstage.*

SCENE THIRTY A: 'DOLL FACE'

Kat's apartment.

EMILY *enters with her doll and shows* RACHEL *how her doll can dance, then hands the doll to* RACHEL. RACHEL *plays along.* EMILY *gives the red nose to* RACHEL. RACHEL *puts on the red nose. They put up their hands and mirror each other. They pull faces together.*

RACHEL (*still wearing the red nose*) *turns and notices the audience. She smiles and waves at them, noticing them for the first time.* EMILY *is unsure what* RACHEL *is doing. She tries to get* RACHEL*'s attention.*

EMILY: Rache Nan?

> RACHEL *playfully shares her doll with her new-found audience, oblivious to* EMILY.

Rache Nan?

> *Beat.*

Can I have a cookie? Rachie Nanna? I know where they are …

> RACHEL *continues to play with the doll, forgetting the audience and* EMILY.

> EMILY *exits.*

> RACHEL *cuddles the doll as if was her baby.*

SCENE THIRTY B: 'NOT READY'

Kat's apartment.

ANGELA *enters and walks towards* RACHEL. ANGELA *begins walking slowly towards the audience, encouraging* RACHEL *to come with her.* ANGELA *points to the audience and looks back to* RACHEL *encouragingly.*

RACHEL *shakes her head and steps back. She begins to inch further away from* ANGELA. ANGELA *watches* RACHEL *move further away.* RACHEL *looks down at her doll, and, happily distracted, she leaves with her doll.*

ANGELA *watches* RACHEL *exit.*

SCENE THIRTY-ONE: 'GOODBYE'

Dementia ward.

MAGGIE *is lying in bed, in a very weakened state.* RACHEL *is by her side, attempting to feed her with a spoon.*

KAT *enters.*

KAT *and* RACHEL *hug hello. Both are wearing masks.*

RACHEL: She's doing better today. A little grumpy. Thanks for coming. I really gotta go. Can I leave her with you?

>KAT *nods and* RACHEL *kisses* KAT *and hands her the spoon.*

[*To* MAGGIE, *hugging her goodbye*] Love ya Mum!

KAT: Are they allowing hugging?

RACHEL: [*to* KAT] Just keep ya mask on. [*To* MAGGIE] Bye, Mum. Love you. Bye Kat …

KAT: [*to* RACHEL] Mum.

RACHEL: Yep?

KAT: I've decided to stay.

RACHEL: They're letting us stay as long as we like now, darling.

KAT: No, I mean. In Canberra. Emily and me.

>*Beat.*

RACHEL: I would love that.

>*Beat.*

I gotta go. Love you both!

>RACHEL *exits.*

KAT: Hi Baggie Nanna. [*Offering her the spoon*] Want some more?

MAGGIE: [*slightly sleepy*] Rachel?

KAT: It's me, Kat.

MAGGIE: Kat? Silly name for a child, Rache.

KAT: Emily said she loved visiting her Baggie Nanna last week. She says to say hi.

MAGGIE: Who?

KAT: Emily? My daughter, Emily. Your great granddaughter.

MAGGIE: When are you going to marry that beau of yours? [*Mumbling*] Whatshisname … Samuel …

KAT: Sammy. Nanna's he's …

She sighs.

Can I get you anything Baggie?

MAGGIE: Ice cream?

MAGGIE closes her eyes,

KAT: I'll see what I can do.

KAT goes to leave, then turns back and looks at MAGGIE sleeping. She sits back down with her.

Hey, Nanna, I'm sorry we didn't … I didn't visit you before. I wanted to be strong for Emily. I thought I could protect her from … Maybe it didn't mean enough to me, because Mum protected *me* from it, and I didn't see it, or want to see it. Whatever. I dunno.

Beat.

I thought daughters and granddaughters shouldn't have to look after mothers, but here we are.

She tries to laugh off tears.

Cursed to care! We're there to watch them grow up, not them watch us grow down. Anyway … I'm … [*Through tears*] I'm sorry. Jeez, it's really hard to cry with this flippin' mask on!

MAGGIE still has her eyes closed. KAT can't hear or see MAGGIE breathing and gets nervous.

Nanna?

MAGGIE: [*mumbling*] Curse is a blessing.

KAT: Yeah.

MAGGIE: Ice cream.

KAT: Okay.

Beat.

MAGGIE: Music?

KAT: [*listening*] I can't hear anything. Do you want me to play or sing something?

MAGGIE *opens her eyes and turns her head to see someone in the distance dancing.* KAT *follows her glance.*

MAGGIE: Why are they … dancing?

KAT: I think it's sweet, Nanna. Maybe they're new, just enjoying a dance.

MAGGIE: [*looking closely at* KAT] Oh, you're that nice carer.

KAT: Kat. It's Kat, Baggie Nan.

MAGGIE: No. That's not it. Kat's coming to take me to the beach soon … We better get up. Come on.

MAGGIE *doesn't move.*

KAT: Nanna, it's okay. We can go to the beach when you're ready.

MAGGIE: [*closing her eyes*] Stupid roundabouts.

KAT: I'm here Nanna. You rest. I'll bring Emily tomorrow, okay?

MAGGIE: Okay.

KAT: Love you Nanna.

MAGGIE: Darling Emily.

Beat.

KAT: I'll look after Rachel, okay?

MAGGIE: Promise?

KAT: I promise.

MAGGIE: Ice cream.

MAGGIE *snores.*

KAT: Yeah, ice cream.

KAT *bends down to kiss* MAGGIE *goodbye and gently removes her hand from* MAGGIE*'s grip and goes to leave.* MAGGIE *opens her eyes but strains to recognise* KAT *with her mask on.* MAGGIE *reaches out her hand and takes* KAT*'s mask off her face.* KAT *assists her.* MAGGIE *smiles in recognition of* KAT*'s face.*

MAGGIE: You still love him?

KAT: Oh, Baggie Nan. [*Holding back tears*] With all my heart.

Beat.

It's been so hard Nanna. I never got to …

MAGGIE: Say goodbye.

KAT: Yeah.

KAT *takes Maggie's hand and holds it as they look at each other.*

MAGGIE: Bye …
KAT: Goodbye.

> KAT *exits.*

MAGGIE: [*almost inaudible*] Kitty Kat.

SCENE THRITY TWO: 'MIRRORED FACES'

Dementia ward.

RACHEL *sits on the bed with a very weak* MAGGIE, *who is propped up slightly, so they meet at eye level.* RACHEL *takes the red nose out of her pocket and gives it back to* MAGGIE.

RACHEL: I believe this is yours.

> RACHEL *gently puts it on* MAGGIE's *face for her.* RACHEL *connects her palms to* MAGGIE's. *They mirror each other with slow hand movements.* MAGGIE *and* RACHEL *turn their faces to the audience, looking out gently. This moment is held until* MAGGIE *leans backward, looking upward, her eyes open. She sighs, her mouth gently open.* RACHEL *removes the red nose, and assists* MAGGIE *to lie back more comfortably, propped up (as in Prologues A and B).* RACHEL *holds* MAGGIE's *hand.*

SCENE THIRTY-THREE: 'ASHES'

Beach.

RACHEL, KAT, *and* EMILY *are all at the beach.*

RACHEL *carries an urn with Maggie's ashes. They pause at the end of the jetty together and look out at the ocean.*

RACHEL *sits down at the end of the jetty.* KAT *and* EMILY *join* RACHEL. RACHEL *opens the urn, and looks at the others who reassure her.*

Together they empty the contents of the urn into the water. They sit and hold each other, looking at the water.

Gradually they all stand and peel off from the jetty. RACHEL *is last to leave and looks back at the water.* KAT *and* EMILY *look back at* RACHEL, *who waves goodbye to the sea. They all walk along the beach.*

RACHEL *breaks away from the others, wandering completely in the wrong direction.* KAT *notices this.* KAT *watches* RACHEL, *waiting for her to notice.* EMILY *also waits.* KAT *calls out to* RACHEL *but is unheard.* KAT *realises there's no-one else. She looks back to* EMILY, *who is happily picking up pebbles and skimming them.* KAT *realises she must go and get* RACHEL. *She takes a deep breath and follows after* RACHEL. *She arrives at* RACHEL*'s side, pauses in front of her and takes her hand and nods gently in the other direction, guiding her back to the right path.* RACHEL *is surprised and disorientated but complies. They both return to join* EMILY.

EMILY *gives a pebble to* RACHEL, *who looks at it, puzzled, then puts it her pocket. They all walk back together, in the right direction, now holding hands.*

We hear a seagull.

RACHEL *watches a seagull pass, mouthing silently 'seagull'.* KAT *notices* RACHEL *wandering off in the wrong direction again.* KAT *follows and pulls* RACHEL *back on track, as they all watch the seagull fly off.* KAT *keeps* RACHEL *close.* EMILY *joins them again. All three hug closely as they walk off the beach together.* RACHEL *attempting one final look up and smile at the seagull, and a wink at the audience.*

Fade to silhouette of women walking along beach together.

THE END

IN THE SUBCONSCIOUS MAZE OF DEMENTIA, HOW DO YOU FIND YOUR WAY HOME?

PLAYWRIGHT: RUTH PIELOOR

DEMENTED

11 - 20 AUGUST | THE Q | **TICKETS $25 - $50**

Demented is the latest work by acclaimed ACT theatre-maker and published playwright (Under My Bed) Ruth Pieloor, who, inspired by her deeply personal experience, turns her magic-realism trademark into an oddly comic, yet breathtaking and touching realisation of Dementia.

An exciting collaboration with local and regional artists, this unique production intercepts playful clowning, exquisite puppetry, dramatic dialogue and an original score, to share a heroine's captivating relationship with dementia.

We meet Rachel — the mother, daughter, carer, lover, artist - and gently take her hand as she unravels new challenges in her family's tapestry of memories, and the legacy it leaves in its wake.

Director: Ali Clinch
Sound Designer: Ruth O'Brien
Puppetry Designer: Hilary Talbot

Dramaturg: Peter Matheson
Lighting Designer: Jacob Acquilina
Starring: Heidi Silberman & Chrissie Shaw

surround

REBUS THEATRE

ACT

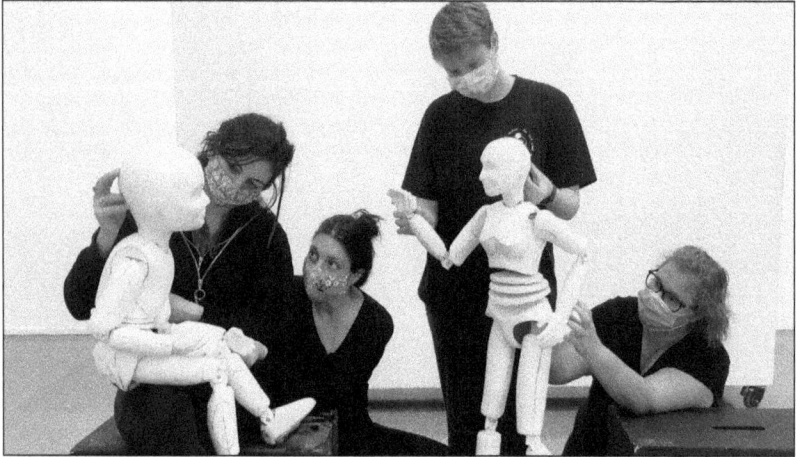

ArtsACT funded development of Demented at Ainslie and Gorman Arts Centres in 2021. Artists: Ylaria Rogers, Heidi Silberman, Kit Berry, Ali Clinch. Puppetry design: Hilary Talbot. Dramaturgy: Peter Matheson. Photo: Ruth Pieloor.

Connecting with my mum, who had advanced dementia, in between lockdowns. Photo: Ruth Pieloor.

PROGRAM INTRODUCTION

In 2018 I launched a new theatre company, Echo Theatre, at The Q. We committed to doing a play a year, drawn from the incredible list of plays written by women. During a newspaper interview at the time I was asked, 'Why are you only programming plays by women? Aren't you ignoring the classics?' My answer: 'I'm not ignoring the classics, I'm finding the new ones.'

Quite apart from the absurdity of the interview question, when the bulk of the theatre's season was still overwhelmingly written by men, is this really the best we can do? To just continue to program the same plays, tell the same stories, and platform the same lives on our stages? I think we need to give our audiences more credit, as well as acknowledge and celebrate the diversity of our theatregoing public. Our patrons want to see themselves on stage, to hear stories that reflect their own experiences, but they are also hungry for difference, to be transported, and to walk in other people's shoes.

When I called for expressions of interest for our newly launched 'Q the Locals' season, I hoped that I would get some interesting stories, something new, something to grow our audience, something to move and challenge and engage. I was overwhelmed by the number of submissions I received, and was thrilled with the variety and quality of the work offered. But when *Demented* came across my desk, I knew I had found something special, a work that would tick every box I had hoped for.

Ruth's script is a sensitive, imaginative, and entirely unique handling of a difficult subject matter. This disease touches so many people's lives, and is part of so many people's experiences, and yet their stories are not often told, as it can be difficult to convince an audience to engage with such heartbreaking material. Ruth's personal experience with dementia, as well as her training in clowning and puppetry, have given her the ability to approach this story with a lightness and a humour that will make it accessible to audiences.

I believe that it is vital to meaningfully support our local artists at all stages of their careers, and I am passionate about programming work from emerging, mid-career, and established creatives from our region. The importance of telling contemporary Australian stories cannot be underestimated, and the ability for new writers to take their work from page to stage is essential to the ongoing development of our regions' ecology of artists.

The incredible team of creatives involved in *Demented*, all at various stages of their careers, bring so much knowledge, skill, and talent to the production. I am proud to be able to support Ruth and her team and to provide a platform for this remarkable work. After production, and publication, I look forward to seeing where it goes next.

Jordan Best
Queanbeyan Performing Arts Centre Artistic Director
Echo Theatre Director-Producer

WRITER'S NOTE

I am always interested in heartfelt stories that move us to both laughter and tears. Stories that question the human condition and the capacity we have, to endure, to love, and to belong to one another. *Demented* was no exception.

My journey as a writer beyond the short form truly began back in 2014 with writer residency development program 'The Hive' at The Street Theatre, Canberra's leading theatre hub for emerging and established artists. After creating and developing my first one-act play *Under My Bed*, published by Australian Plays Transform, I felt more ready to try my hand at a full-length work. Encouraged by Shelly Higgs and Caroline Stacey, I set out to develop the work independently with arguably Australia's leading dramaturg, Peter Matheson. It was surely this connection and undying support that allowed me to win a local government arts grant to develop the work further. I was on my way.

Much to the surprise and perhaps even reluctance of some, I was keen to explore the theme and nature of dementia through the unusual use of comedy, via clowning. This was largely influenced by my work as a Clown Doctor in children's wards at the Canberra Hospital, which I thank my training and engagement with The Humour Foundation for. I have immense gratitude for The Clown Institute's Alicia Gonzales for her deeply encouraging endorsement that humour of this nature can connect with audiences in such a sensitive way. And when Jordan Best, artistic director of Queanbeyan Performing Arts Centre, understood and celebrated my vision for this play, I felt seen.

I felt I had arrived as a producer and a writer. Following my Q Theatre application success, I was accepted to be published with Currency Press, which only now as I write this, makes me feel I can truly call myself a playwright.

But the person who provided the greatest inspiration for *Demented* is my dearest mother, also a published writer, Janette Pieloor. During the times of caring for her in her home, before we truly embraced it for what it was, leading up to and after diagnosis, learning about dementia, unlearning tasks, reeling from paperwork, frustrations, family tensions, and all the waiting for support, I took notes.

Many of the details have been extended and altered (never let the truth get in the way of a good story!) including changing the gender of the characters, as I only have sons. But I felt the work was a mother-daughter tale, and stronger as a woman's story. So often caring falls to the female, and for the ACT dementia is currently the leading cause of death in women. I have been influenced by others too, who, sadly, also connected deeply with experiencing dementia. Every scene, indeed, almost every interaction, owes its inspiration to a real-life journey of dementia.

So why comedy, and why clowning? In the last couple of years of Mum's life, we discovered ever-present, honest, playful, creative, healing, age-irrelevant, and even spiritual connections. Through such communications of the heart, we found laughter, tears, song, dance, babble, and nonsensical child's 'play'. We took each other on imaginative journeys, creating our own memories and reinventing old ones. I believe we did this with as much love, gusto and fulfilment a mother and daughter relationship could ever hope for, given the circumstances. And I believe as challenging a condition as dementia is, we played it as best we could right to its final curtain.

This was not only my mother's journey, but her sister's, and her mother's. Perhaps if I live long enough to tell the tale, it will be mine too.

Ruth Pieloor

Playwright and producer

DIRECTOR'S NOTE

I spent five difficult years caring for my father who became unwell when I was a first-time mum. Caring for my son and father simultaneously was both fulfilling and heartbreaking. As one brain capacity would develop, the other was destroyed by Alzheimer's Disease. In this experience, which as I write this, is still very raw, I was struck by the many opportunities for play, by the 'comedy of errors' brought about by living with dementia and the many blessings that this dual role gave me.

Ruth Pieloor approached me to direct a creative development of *Demented* in 2021, several months after my father's death and I was immediately drawn to bringing this story to life on stage. Culturally, there is much to explore with regards to the role of the carer: how we look after our aging parents, and how we might include our children or grandchildren, the playful generation, in their care.

I am drawn to use theatre to explore the gift that dementia brings to those impacted by it. There are many moments in the journey of dementia that words alone cannot capture. Pieloor's inclusion of puppetry and clowning brings great depth to the world of the play and our perception of dementia. It emphasises the different realities experienced by those living with it.

Within the heartache there is joy.

The purest joy, that can come from experiencing something for the first time. Pieloor's work cleverly interweaves the clown's presence into the experience of dementia in a respectful way to remind the audience that there is much to be gained from entering the demented person's reality instead of pushing against it and dragging them back into our world.

Directing work during a pandemic has added complexities. The notion 'the show must go on' is no longer viable and so we work to pivoting endlessly to accommodate these new uncertain times. It has opened the arts up to creative alternatives to understudies, swings, and online rehearsals. Ironically, the flexibility required during a pandemic is not dissimilar to that of the carer: sudden and unpredictable change was the only inevitable as we shaped the play for the stage.

We know It takes a village to raise a child or to care for an elder and also to bring a production to the stage. There are many people who have offered support to bring this vision to life. I thank the people in my creative and personal life who have enabled *Demented* to reach this point. A special mention to my husband, Stafford, and son Charlie who must make sacrifices in their lives to enable me to reach my full potential in my work. Thank you.

What a great gift the Q locals program gives in ensuring that women's stories and experiences are not overlooked by the theatre world. Pieloor's play explores the complex high stakes that face many contemporary Australian women.

Ali Clinch

Demented Director

(Acting with Ali
www.actingwithali.com)

RUTH PIELOOR
PLAYWRIGHT / PRODUCER

Ruth Pieloor is grateful to be a 'Q the Locals' recipient as producer to premiere her first full length play *Demented*. Ruth's first love was in performance, having trained and worked with Terrapin Puppet Theatre, BA in Acting at Theatre Nepean (UWS), and now working as an established local actor, improv artist, puppeteer, director, and tutor, who facilitates theatre devising and performance skills workshops in communities, corporate settings, schools, and for adults with disabilities. Ruth has conceived, directed, and written countless performances, including for ATYP, Canberra Youth Theatre, ricochet working productions, Short and Sweet, Rebus Theatre, ImproACT, and with a multitude of private and public schools and colleges in Sydney, Canberra and regional NSW. Ruth has performed in various theatre productions at The Street Theatre, in local short films, is a current Playback ensemble member with Rebus Theatre, resident Clown Doctor with The Humour Foundation at The Canberra Hospital, tutor with ImproACT, and proud MEAA Ambassador. As an emerging playwright and producer, Ruth has received numerous awards for her short plays with Short and Sweet, and in 2017 her one-act play *Under My Bed*, developed and supported by ArtsACT and Ainslie and Gorman Arts Centres, was published with Australian Plays Transform. Ruth was resident writer-producer with The Street Theatre's 'Hive' and 'Expand' programs, and in 2021 was an ArtsACT recipient as writer-producer to develop *Demented* with dramaturg Peter Matheson, supported by Ainslie and Gorman Arts Centres. Ruth is a Canberra local, passionate about inspiring and encouraging artists to support one another, to strengthen and diversify arts practices.

ALI CLINCH
DIRECTOR

Ali Clinch is an award-winning actor and director winning the Reclink 'Spirit Award' for her work as Artistic Director of Acting Crazy Theatre in 2010, and most recently the 'Canberra Critics Circle Award' for her work on *What if Scientists Ruled the World*, commissioned by the Australian Academy of Science. Ali specialises in 'applied theatre', working with people to help them explore their stories theatrically. Honours graduate of Griffith University's Bachelor of Applied Theatre, Ali's most recent directorial projects include *Titanic 2020*, a play by and for senior Canberrans Pandemic Players, exploring their experience with Covid-19, funded by ACT Health in collaboration with COTA ACT and Rebus Theatre; *Chemical Reaction*, commissioned by Questacon; *Mothering Father*, a play exploring the personal experience of being a carer to a parent with dementia, National Film & Sound Archives and Smith's Alternative; and she also co-wrote and co-directed Rebus Theatre's *A Tender Thing*. Ali is programs manager, drama tutor, actor, and 'Playback Theatre' ensemble member with Rebus Theatre. She runs 'Acting with Ali' to empower and upskill local talent in Queanbeyan and ACT.

PETER MATHESON
DRAMATURG

Since becoming a freelance dramaturg in 2002, Peter Matheson has assessed scripts and/or worked dramaturgically with most of the major mainstage (as well as many smaller) theatre companies and all the assessment agencies in Australia. He has taught playwrighting, handled residencies, facilitated development programs and tutored in organizations from tertiary institutions through to enthusiastic amateurs. His most recent work has been with TasPerforms, Playlab's 'Incubator' series, Blue Cow's 'Cowshed' program, and Yirra Yaakin Theatre in Perth.

CHRISSIE SHAW
MAGGIE

Chrissie Shaw has performed in Sydney revues, children's theatre, and folksinging since the 1960s. She toured Australia with TIE company Pipi Storm, co-created shows, and ran workshops with children and young people, toured *The Dresses*, *The Not Too Late Show*, and performed with TAU Theatre, Women on a Shoestring, Jigsaw Theatre, and The Street Theatre to name a few. She co-created, and performed in *About Face*, *Footprints on the Wind*, *A Sweeter Fern—That's Red!*, *Drumming on Water*, *The Keeper*, and touring children's shows *Flotsam and Jetsam*, and *Gran's Bag*. The Street Theatre productions include *Violine*, *Lawrie and Shirley*, and *Bijou*, which toured nationally to sell-out audiences. Children's shows *The Man Whose Mother was a Pirate*, and *Arborio*, appeared at the Sydney Opera House, also *Pearl Verses the World*, and *Rolling Home*, the latter visiting Riverside Theatres. Chrissie conducts choirs, performs role-plays for ANU medical students, and has won many awards including Canberra Critics' Circle and Green Room awards. Chrissie is a proud member of MEAA Actors Equity.

HEIDI SILBERMAN
RACHEL

Heidi Silberman is an award-winning Canberra-based performer, director, writer and educator. Scripted performances include in Lakespeare's *As You Like It*, *Richard III*, *A Midsummer Night's Dream*, Couching Giraffe's *The Penelopiad*, Limbo Theatre's *The Good Doctor*, and Moral Panic's *Love/Chamberlain*. Heidi created and directed Lightbulb Improv's productions *Under the Bonnet* and *Shakespeare Off the Ruff*. She has created, directed and performed in improvised shows: *Bridesquad*, *Shakespeare with Zombies*, *Femme Noire*, and *The Home Front*, which had successful seasons in Canberra, Adelaide Fringe

Festival and in regional NSW. She also co-wrote and co-directed Rebus Theatre's *A Tender Thing*. Heidi is co-founder of Chrysalis Theatre, co-producer of the Canberra Unscripted Festival, and her alter ego is Dr Peek-a-boo, a Clown Doctor with The Humour Foundation.

RACHEL PENGILLY
KAT

Rachel Pengilly is an award-winning actor and a UC graduate (BA) in Acting (Chancellor's Award). Rachel has worked extensively across film and theatre. She made her professional stage debut in 2021 as Lizzie in Echo Theatre's *Wolf Lullaby*. Other stage credits include Bare Witness' *I Have No Enemies*. Screen credits include *Comments*, *Bullying is a Crime*, and *The Melody*, awarding her Best Supporting Actress. Rachel was a resident artist at Belco Arts Centre in 2021 for her play *Legacies* and is one of the Q Theatre's Young Ambassadors in 2022. A wearer of many hats, Rachel is also a playwright, stage manager, high-school drama teacher, scenic artist, surfer, and proud dog-mum. Rachel has been a proud MEAA member since 2021.

CAROLYN ECCLES
EMILY

Carolyn Eccles is a multi-disciplinary artist and arts educator working across movement/performance, visual arts and the written word. She is one half of the collaborative visual arts practice, darkroom, a member of performance group Luca's Daughter's and an associate artist for the performance company, Lingua Franca. Carolyn has been performing for over 15 years and has trained in Suzuki, Viewpoints, Butoh and Contact Improvisation. She toured seven shows nationally as an ensemble and solo Theatre in Education performer for five years, and has appeared at folk festivals across the country. She holds a Graduate Certificate in Arts and Community Engagement from the VCA.

FIONA LEACH
COSTUME DESIGNER

Fiona Leach has worked as a costume designer for over 20 years with many Canberra theatre companies. Her most recent design was for Free Rain Theatre's production of *Priscilla Queen of the Desert*. In the past five years local productions include: *Mamma Mia, Cat on a Hot Tin Roof, Absurd Person Singular, The Little Mermaid, To Kill a Mockingbird, Kinky Boots, The World Goes Round, Once Upon a Mattress, 42nd Street, 12 Angry Men, Shrek, Alice in Wonderland, Radio on Repertory, Les Miserables, The History Boys, The 39 Steps*, and *The Summer of the Seventeenth Doll*. Fiona has received multiple CAT (Canberra Area Theatre) Awards for costume design in various musicals and in 2017 Fiona was awarded the prestigious 'Silver CAT' Award in recognition of her achievements in costume design.

BRETT OLZEN
AUSLAN INTERPRETER

Brett Olzen is a CODA (Child of Deaf Adults) who grew up in a Deaf family and is the only native-speaking Auslan interpreter in Canberra. Brett has worked as an Auslan interpreter for 25 years in education, community and the arts. His work has included conferences, performances, theatre productions (including with Rebus Theatre), computer access programs and guided tours at the National Gallery of Australia. He is a founding member of the Deaf Dance Group with Belconnen Arts Centre. Brett's work has seen him interpret with territory and federal government, with various prime ministers, the Dalai

Lama, and at multiple ACT Chief Minister's Inclusion Awards, including when he himself was as a finalist for the 'Life-Time Achievement in Supporting People with Disability Award' in 2019. Brett is passionate about supporting events and programs to be more accessible and inclusive.

MEL DAVIES
SET DESIGNER / STAGE MANAGER

Mel Davies commenced her theatrical career in the early 1990s, working with Canberra Philharmonic and Canberra Rep doing backstage crew, lighting, and sound, while spending her days at WIN Television as a news camera assistant. Mel has developed her career in theatre through Canberra Opera doing set design and stage management for *Die Fledermaus*, *Cosi Fan Tutte*, *Gianni Schicchi*, *Cavelleria Rusticana* (2019), and with The National Opera's *La Clemeza Di Tito* (2021) processes.

LACHLAN DAVIES
SET CONSTRUCTION / ASSISTANT STAGE MANAGER

Lachlan Davies graduated Year 12 last year with Certificate II in woodwork and furniture-making and is developing a career in set design and construction. Lachlan spent his teenage years learning the ropes of theatre as a lighting operator and assistant set construction for Canberra Opera's *Die Fledermaus*, *Cosi Fan Tutte*, *Gianni Schicchi*, *Cavalleria Rusticana* (2019) and was lead set builder The National Opera's *La Clemenza Di Tito* (2021).

JACOB AQUILINA
LIGHTING DESIGNER, LIGHTING AND SOUND OPERATOR

Jacob Aquilina is a young up and coming lighting designer, who has a theatrical lighting background working on plays and musical theatre in our region. Jacob is proud to be Eclipse Lighting and Sound's Technical Manager for The Q Theatre Queanbeyan Performing Arts Centre. Some of Jacob's recent favourite theatrical credits include Echo Theatre's *Wolf Lullaby*, Supa Production's *Full Monty*, and Queanbeyan Players' *Oliver*. He is always wanting to upskill himself and work on the wide range of events.

DAMIAN ASHCROFT
SOUND DESIGNER

Damian Ashcroft has been involved with Canberra's arts scene for over a decade. He earned an A.Dip (Music) from CIT in 2014, winning Student of the Year. After graduating he began performing regularly with Ruth O'Brien, collaborating on her debut EP, *Invaluable* (2018). In 2016 he rekindled his interest in theatre at ImproACT. Damian began teaching improvised theatre in 2019 and directed the show *Adventures* at Canberra Unscripted in the same year. These days Damian weaves his love of fantasy, improvised theatre and music production into the *Surrealia* podcast, which is currently in production for its fourth season

RUTH O'BRIEN
SOUND ASSISTANT

Ruth O'Brien is a singer, songwriter, and multi-passionate creative. Founder of *Upbeat*, a newsletter promoting and creating opportunities for Canberra musicians and industry workers, Ruth regularly interviews and writes for *BMA Magazine*, is on the advisory group for Rebus Theatre, is on the board of the National Live Music Awards, and works as a creative freelancer, lending her skills and voice to many initiatives and projects across the ACT arts scene. Ruth has worked in many disability arts projects over the past five years including as a sound designer and actor of Rebus Theatre, as an accessibility advisor for Accessible Arts NSW, and consultant on a range of Disability Inclusion Action Plans (DIAPs) and projects for many local cultural institutions. Ruth is developing her second album, and is delighted to work on this project with this amazing group of Canberra-based artists.

HILARY TALBOT
PUPPET DESIGNER

Hilary Talbot is a Canberra-based artist and sculptor working with a diverse range of materials to create three-dimensional works. She has a special interest in puppetry and visual theatre, having designed and made a wide variety of puppets and props for local and national theatre productions, performance artists, and cultural institutions. Hilary also has her own art practice, with two recent solo exhibitions: *Glimpses Of A Seagull Flying Blind* at The Pinnacles Gallery, Townsville (2018), and *The Piano Creatures: A Ragged Shore* at the Canberra Museum and Gallery, Canberra (2021).

ROBIN DAVIDSON
CLOWN COACH

Robin Davidson is an actor, clown, director, teacher, and writer. He is the founding artistic director of Rebus Theatre. A graduate of Charles Sturt University in Theatre/Media, with first class honours, Robin has taught in East Timor, Thailand, and Sri Lanka. Robin was co-awarded the 2005 Media Entertainment and Arts Alliance ACT 'Green Room Award'. In 2019 he studied for three months full-time in the Pedagogy of Movement Theatre in Italy with Giovanni Fusetti. Robin has also appeared as an unusually large bogong moth, a giant mango, and a seal.

ACKNOWLEDGEMENTS

We would like to acknowledge the traditional custodians and original artists of the Ngambri and Ngunnawal lands, where development, rehearsals, and the premiere performance of *Demented* took place. We give thanks, and pay respects to indigenous Elders; past, present and emerging. Always was, always will be, Aboriginal land.

SPECIAL THANKS

Karla Conway, Shelly Higgs, Caroline Stacey, Craig Alexander, Pete Pieloor, Alicia Gonzales, Ben Drysdale, Liz Drysdale, Anne Murn, Ariana Odermatt, Rochelle Whyte, Stefanie Lekkas, Adelaide Rief, Goldele Rayment, Suzanne Rogers, Goran Srejic, Greg Lee, Mike Hennessey, Brad McCusker, Jordan Best, Natasha Vickery, Joel Horwood, Victoria Hopkins, Ylaria Rogers, Kit Berry, Lynn Petersen, Jane Duong, Bill Stephens, Claire Grady, Jodine Muir, Katie Pollock, Victoria Jackson, Chris Stanilewicz, Femke Withag, Yolande Norris, Richard Hale, Ethan Lewis, Kangara Waters, IRT, and Free-Rain Theatre Company.

SUPPORTED BY

Supported by

ACT Government

THE Q
QUEANBEYAN
PERFORMING
ARTS
CENTRE

GNCL
D'ARSUG

REBUS
THEATRE

TINY'S PRODUCTIONS

surround

RH METAL CONCEPTS
Proudly Australian Made